Right Here Right NOW!

Living the Anointed Life
With Jesus and HIS Family

CONTENTS

PARADISE FORGOTTEN: CHRISTIANITY GETS RELIGIOUS

CHRISTENDOM AT THE NEW MILLENNIUM

RIGHT HERE, RIGHT NOW!

BIBLIOGRAPHY

NOTES

Now to Him who is able to do immeasurably more than all we ask or imagine, according to His power that is at work within us, to Him be glory in the church and in Christ Jesus throughout all generations, for ever and ever! Amen.

1

PARADISE LOST: LIFE WITHOUT GOD

Imagine No Religion

Imagine walking with God. Literally…

It's evening in your garden world. The warmth of the afternoon lingers in the meadow in front of you, but behind you a cool, fragrant breeze stirs the darkening woods. The sun, riding low in the sky, floods the landscape with gold. Soon it will paint a masterpiece over the western hills. Your senses take in the beauty, and your heart appreciates it, yet these wonders cannot explain the joyful expectancy that wells up like a song in your soul. There is another reason for it.

He is coming. Soon!

The Person who created you has promised to meet you here. He often comes during the evening, because He knows it is *your* favorite time for a walk. As you walk together, He shows you many things—canyons, mountains, oceans, fields, and all the creatures that call these wild regions home. Each moment with your Friend is tinged with discovery and wonder. But the greatest marvel of all is always simply *Him*. He is deeper than any canyon, grander than any mountain, mightier than any ocean, gentler and more inviting than any meadow, yet wilder than any of His creatures. He is your delight, and you are His. You call Him Father, and He calls you His child.

He is not like you. Yet somehow—amazingly—*you* are a bit like *Him*. He speaks to you often of your role in this Paradise. You, together with the mate that He has given you, are to nurture and rule it as His representatives. It is a staggering responsibility, yet you are unafraid, for He will always be there to teach and guide you. You are totally dependent on Him, yet content. He is all you need.

It has never occurred to you to feel frightened or guilty about meeting with Him. You certainly never find Him dull or boring! You never feel "religious." In fact, it is doubtful that anyone could ever really explain the concept of a religion to you, even if they tried.

You have never "said a prayer," let alone "chanted," though you often speak with Him.

You have never organized a choir, though you often sing to Him—just as He often sings to you.

You have never given a speech about Him, though you often speak lovingly of Him to the helper that He made for you and even to the beasts of the field when you encounter them.

He is the central fact of your existence. You quite literally couldn't live without Him. It has never even crossed your mind to try. Your life is already rich with meaning and bursting with adventure. No wonder you are waiting so expectantly for Him now!

Does that picture of life sound good to you? It should.

You were created for it.

Anatomy of the Fall

We all know how the tragedy played out: Adam and Eve sinned and lost Paradise. In its place they received—in a sense, they created—a fallen world cursed with hard labor, painful childbirth, difficult relationships, and in the end, death. You may have been created for Paradise, but you certainly weren't born into it. Sin is the reason.

But why on earth did Adam and Eve do it? How could they have been so foolish? They had it so good—perfect, in fact. How could the devil deceive them? The answer to that question sums up the sad history of our fallen species.

Let's read the account. You've heard it many times before, no doubt, but have you ever really noticed the devil's strategy?

> He said to the woman, "Did God really say, 'You must not eat from any tree in the garden'?"
>
> The woman said to the serpent, "We may eat fruit from the trees in the garden, but God did say, 'You must not eat fruit from the tree that is in the middle of the garden, and you must not touch it, or you will die.'"
>
> "You will not surely die," the serpent said to the woman. "For God knows that when you eat of it your eyes will be opened, and you will be like God, knowing good and evil."
>
> When the woman saw that the fruit of the tree was good for food and pleasing to the eye, and also desirable for gaining wisdom, she took some and ate it. She also gave some to her husband, who was with her, and he ate it. (Genesis 3:2-6)

What, then, was the bait on the devil's hook? *The prospect of an independent existence without a moment-by-moment need for God.* "God's holding out on you. He knows that your eyes will be opened if you pursue the knowledge of good and evil. You won't need Him to tell you what to do. You'll be wise enough to decide things for yourself. In fact, you can be your own gods!"

Independence was the intoxicating bait. Unfortunately, independence is exactly what humanity got out of the bargain. And it was certainly not much of a bargain! Within a few decades of going it alone and deciding for themselves what seemed good, the first human parents had raised themselves a murderer. Within a few centuries, starvation, war, cruelty, hatred, deceit, and exploitation had appeared on the scene—everything humanity has strived so unsuccessfully to eliminate from their civilizations as the millennia pass by.

Independence wasn't supposed to turn out that way, at least according to the snake. Somehow when he spoke of it, it sounded *exciting*. Intelligent. Important. Sophisticated. But he had "forgotten" to mention a crucial fact: *independence* always means *separation*. And separation from God is neither exciting nor intelligent.

Ever since that first temptation, our species has absolutely *craved* independence from God and has paid the price of separation from Him to get it. We still like the looks of that forbidden fruit, despite the heartache it has brought us. Like the subjects in Jesus' parable of the ten minas, we consider the prospects of submitting to God and cry, "We do not want Him to be our King" (Luke 19:14). Most humans, it seems, want a god, but they want one who will be satisfied with token religious observances and then leave them alone so that they can lead their *own* lives their *own* way.

Humanity in Hiding

How did Adam and Eve react once they ate the fruit? Again, let's try to read the account as if the ink were still fresh on the page:

> Then the eyes of both of them were opened, and they realized they were naked; so they sewed fig leaves together and made coverings for themselves. Then the man and his wife heard the sound of the LORD God as He was walking in the garden in the cool of the day, and they hid from the LORD God among the trees of the garden. But the LORD God called to the man, "Where are you?"
>
> He answered, "I heard You in the garden, and I was afraid because I was naked; so I hid." (Genesis 3:7-11)

Adam and Eve's *first* reaction after sinning was to *hide from God.* Sin had given them new instincts, like self-consciousness, self-preservation, and the fear of punishment. Suddenly they felt so very *separate* from God. So they hid—and humanity has been in hiding ever since.

The fallen man and woman knew, of course, that hiding from God in any physical sense was impossible, so they crawled out from the woods and faced Him when He called. But they kept hiding nonetheless. The difference was that now, instead of taking refuge behind the thickest tree trunks they could find, they hid behind a forest of excuses, blame-shifting, and half-truths.

In the end, God had no choice but to fulfill His word and to give the first humans the independence and separation they craved. Now *He* hid Himself from *them.* Before, they had enjoyed unbroken intimacy and friendship with Him. That relationship came to an abrupt halt. The Tree of Life, whose fruit could have extended the friendship for eternity, was hidden from their sight forever.

Within a generation, the human race was a living, breathing disaster. Killers begat killers, and then the killers got organized and began building the first cities and civilizations. It was "at that time," the Genesis account tells us, that "men began to call on the name of the LORD" (Genesis 4:26). The world was still young; Adam and Eve were still alive. But because it was no longer possible to walk with God (literally) as they once had, human civilization created a substitute:

Religion.

Ever since that day, humans have tried to have it both ways—to appease God through ritualized service, yet to maintain an independence from Him in practical terms. Those goals might seem contradictory. But religion was an ingenious invention, because it made both goals seem quite possible. How? By dividing life neatly into two distinct categories, the *religious* and the *secular.* The religious was relegated to certain special times and places, with certain expert holy men to serve both as a link and a buffer between God and man. The secular side of life was now free to receive the lion's share of man's attention.

Human culture shot off in a thousand different directions after God's intervention at Babel. Languages, foods, clothing, and customs developed in an amazing diversity of ways. Religion developed right along with them. But no matter what the external trappings, certain constants have remained, from nation to nation, crossing the oceans and spanning the globe. Religion still sets aside certain places, days, and people as "holier" or "more special" than the rest.

"Special Places"

Virtually every religion known to man has certain buildings or sites designated as especially holy places. Their names may change between cultures, but their function stays the same.

Many religions have constructed buildings called "temples" or the like. Historically, men have often thought of them as housing a particular "deity." Temples literally put God in a box! We have grown a bit more sophisticated since then, or so we think. Men nowadays regard temples more as structures devoted to religious activities.

One very popular religion has temples known as *Gurdwara*. You are welcome to visit one if you agree to a few simple requirements. As you enter, remove the shoes from your feet and place a hat something like a bandana on your head. Leave any cigarettes or alcohol at home; no intoxicants are allowed. After you enter, walk slowly to a chair where the religion's sacred book is enthroned. Bow humbly before the book and then make a monetary offering. You, along with all who are attending the temple, then sit cross-legged on the floor and raise your cupped hands to receive from the ushers a wafer of bread made from sweetened flour and butter.

That's the custom of the fifth largest religion on the planet today. Really, though, virtually all religions have a similar kind of temple, with some comparable ritual to go with it. People have built a variety of religiously purposed buildings—temples, to be sure, but also monasteries, mounds, multistory towers, and elaborate edifices with ornate domes and prayer towers.

"Special places" can be enormous. The outer wall of a temple in Cambodia encloses 203 acres (nearly a square kilometer)! Other "special places" can be quite small. Many religions have constructed "shrines." These structures usually hold a relic or image that people worship or honor. Especially committed religious folk may even construct a yard shrine devoted to a particular "deity" or "saint" outside their home. In the northern Midwest of the United States, "bathtub Madonnas," with a religious statue sheltered in an upended, half-buried bathtub, are a familiar type of yard shrine.

Despite the differences in scale, there is a common purpose for these structures. They are a place people can *attend* when they want to "do" their religious duty.

It's fascinating that many people naturally recognize the similarity of all "religiously purposed buildings," regardless of the religion. In Southeast Asia, for example, the word *wat* can refer to almost any "place of worship." A *wat cheen,* for example, is a building used for Chinese religions, whether Buddhist or Taoist. A *wat khaek* is a structure used by Hindus. A *wat kris* is a building used by Christians. Truly, "out of the overflow of the heart the mouth speaks," for to a Thai, a *wat* is a *wat* is a *wat,* no matter what religion constructed it. If you want to get close to God (whatever your concept of Him), you attend the *wat* of your choice. In contrast, if you want to pursue secular interests, you just steer clear from any *wats* until you are ready to be religious.

Mankind, then, has felt a universal urge to build "sacred" buildings and even to designate specific rivers, mountains, or groves of trees as particularly "holy." It really cannot be denied that special places are a trademark of human religion. But is that really such a bad thing?

Well, please consider this: The very process of setting aside a certain place as "holy" automatically categorizes all other places as somehow *less* holy. If the "holy" belongs to God, then who owns the rest? If a few places are devoted to religious life, what are most places dedicated to? And if you really feel like you are "entering the presence of God" when you go into a certain geographic location, then what does it mean when you *leave?*

What we are saying is that religion simultaneously aims at two goals—allowing humans to draw near to God when they choose, while keeping Him at a safe distance when that's what they would prefer. Designating some places as "special" is one crucial way religion compartmentalizes life.

"Special Times"

Religion not only sets up "sacred" and "secular" categories to divide up the three dimensions of space; it does exactly the same thing for the fourth dimension, time. Certain blocks of time— whether hours in a day, days in a week, or seasons in a year—are counted "special."

We could pick any religion as an example, but we'll choose a relatively new one. During the middle years of the nineteenth century, a 25-year old merchant, claiming to be a prophet, took on a name meaning "the Gate" in his language. The local religious leaders brutally suppressed his new movement, eventually executing him by a firing squad. Soon afterwards, however, a new, even more popular "prophet" emerged from the movement. He claimed to be the "promised one" foretold not only by "the Gate," but supposedly by all "faiths." His teachings would form the foundation of a new religion.

In this system, Friday is set aside as a special day of worship. In addition, there are several designated "holy days" each year. On the spring equinox, for instance, adherents get together for a potluck dinner followed by prayers and readings. Then there are a series of days commemorating the founders of the religion—their birthdays, the days they declared themselves prophets, and the days they died. Finally, there is a winter festival when members typically exchange gifts.

Maybe you've heard of this religion; maybe you haven't. But either way, if the whole holiday scene sounds recognizable, it should. The religions you are more familiar with (including the one you were raised in, most likely) have a "sacred calendar" that differs more in detail than in substance from what you've just read.

Many religions set aside a particular day of the week as special. For the members of one, any religious acts performed on Friday receive a greater reward, because God created Adam on a Friday. The members of another disagree: they observe the day *after* Adam's creation as especially significant. Billions of human beings instead observe *Thursday* as their special day. As in the example of "The Gate," many religions base their holidays around special events in the life of their founder. Similarly, many religions hold festivals on the first day of the year (as they define it) or at some other point in the solar or lunar cycles. Each holy day has its own culture of traditional observances, with meals, gifts, parades, religious services, decorations, and the like.

Even those who ignore the tenets of a particular faith 364 days a year may still observe its "holiest" day. And even events or historical figures far outside the mainstream tenets of the religion may eventually get a day in their honor. For example, several liberal religious bodies in the United States began in 2006 the practice of celebrating "evolution day" on the Sunday closest to the birthday of Charles Darwin! The impulse to designate certain arbitrary days as "sacred" is still universal, even in our sophisticated "post-modern" era. As a comedian once quipped, "I was an atheist once, but I quit. No holidays."

Again, we may ask whether the holy-day habit is really so bad, since everyone seems to do it. What can it hurt? And again, we can answer that the very choice to designate a small number of things—whether geographic locations or days of the year—as "sacred" automatically creates another category for *everything else.* If one day is "most special," what does that make every other day? If one day is set aside as *uniquely* belonging to God, then who has ownership of the rest of the days, *really?* Like special places, special times have the effect—whether consciously intended or not—of compartmentalizing life.

"Special Men"

As we have seen, religion can be a relentless categorizer of places and times. But there is another commodity that it sorts into the "sacred" and the "secular": human beings. For just as human religion picks certain locations on the map or pages on the calendar to be "sacred," it also chooses certain faces in the crowd to be especially "holy."

"Primitive" or tribal cultures have specific men or women who are designated as oracles and shamans—or, to be less politically correct, witchdoctors and medicine men. They are thought to be more in touch with the spirit-world than an average person can be. As a result, they typically are believed to have special powers to heal diseases or change the weather. One such religion calls its shamans "clever men" or "clever women." Besides healing and intercession with the spirit world, these "clever ones" are involved in initiation rites and other secret ceremonies. They enforce tribal laws and are feared for their supposed ability to put an offender to death by singing a magical chant. As you move from culture to culture, many of the details may change, but the basic role of shaman remains the same.

As societies get a bit more organized, religious experts usually take on the full function of "priests." Like shamans, priests are supposed to maintain a special connection to the deity of that religion. Their job description is expanded, however. It now includes performing the correct rituals and counseling common people on religious questions. Priests usually require specialized training or education. Typically they are financially supported. The exact job description for priests varies with each religion, but their functions are often surprisingly familiar, even to an outsider. Regardless of their affiliation, priests in western countries may teach religion classes, put out newsletters, perform weddings and funerals, serve as chaplains in the military or in prisons, and even call themselves by the title "Reverend."

Throughout history, priesthood has had its perks. Centuries ago, one country developed a rigid, hierarchical caste system. Members of the very bottom caste were forced to perform all of the dangerous and unsanitary jobs for the society and in return they suffered strict segregation and desperate poverty. The priests, in contrast, found themselves at the top of the heap. In return for performing the "marrying and burying" rituals for society, they enjoyed the highest standard of living and received the most respect of any of its castes. This caste system can still be found today.

You may not live in a society with a recognized caste system. Regardless, most cultures still have designated "specialists" who are supposed to help common folk understand and fulfill divine requirements. But a "connector" can also be a "separator." That's a real problem when the person you're separated from is God, and the person standing between you and Him is just another man. Yet every society, every religion, has chosen "holy" men and women to play the role of go-between. Why?

Humanity is still hiding from God! Most of us don't really want to get *too* close to Him. He might interfere with our precious "right" (as we see it) to be our *own* gods. And when it comes right down to it, we are rather frightened of Him. We have a nagging sense that He is angry and might just do something rash if we are standing too close! Yet we still realize that we need Him to bless us during life's milestones, like birth, coming of age, and marriage, and to rescue or at least comfort us during life's crises, like illness, famine, or the death of a loved one. Religion offers a solution to the dilemma. It chooses someone to get close to God on our behalf, so he or she can take most of the risks for us while obtaining for us some of God's blessing.

The Hidden Cost of Religion

At first glance, religion may seem like one of mankind's most ingenious inventions. But powerful new inventions can often have unintended disastrous effects. What of religion?

To answer that question, we must think back to humanity *before* the fall. In those glorious days, Adam walked with God face-to-face. He needed no holy place, because every place was filled with the wonder and awe of God's presence. He needed no holy day, for each moment was alive with the consciousness of God. And He needed no holy man to stand between them. As man, Adam took his rightful place, submitting to and learning from his Creator without reservation or fear. He dealt with God directly—as a creature deals with a Creator, to be sure, but also as a dearly loved son deals with a perfectly loving Father.

Mankind lost all of that in the fall.

Has human religion regained what was lost in the fall? Has it satisfied *your* soul—for real? Or has it mostly offered a substitute for the reality that Adam experienced in the garden not so long ago? Do you really want your life compartmentalized, with a few special times, places, or men placed in the "sacred" category and the rest placed in the "secular"?

What if instead God gave you a second chance at the Tree of Life? What if He offered to restore the moment-by-moment peace and friendship and life that Adam squandered?

Would you have the courage to take Him up on it?

2

GOD'S PERFECT RELIGION

Candles in the Darkness

When Adam and Eve took the path of independence, deciding for *themselves* what was "good" or "evil," they fell. Hard. With them fell the human race's hope for a free, unhindered, face-to-face walk with their Creator. Humanity's little experiment with self-rule soon brought chaos and death into every aspect of existence on planet earth. As Paul later put it, "Creation was subjected to frustration…in bondage to decay" (Romans 8:20-21). Everything just fell apart.

God found Himself combating human evil continually. He took drastic measures at times just to keep the species from creating hell on earth. God scattered mankind over the entire planet, confusing their languages so that people couldn't band together to accomplish their twisted goals. He drastically reduced the human lifespan from over 900 years to 120, so that He wouldn't have to "put up with humans for such a long time" (Genesis 6:3). At one point God even took the most radical step imaginable: He wiped out almost the entire species, starting over with one man's family. Still, man's evil could only be restrained, barely—never cured.

And so we read in Genesis some of the saddest words in the Bible: "The Lord observed the extent of human wickedness on the earth, and He saw that everything they thought or imagined was consistently and totally evil. So the Lord was sorry He had ever made them and put them on the earth. It broke His heart" (Genesis 6:5-6).

But in this darkness we find a few—a very few—shining lights.

First came Enoch. We know almost nothing about him, but we do know this: "Enoch *walked with God*; then he was no more, because God took him away" (Genesis 5:24).

Three generations later came Noah. He "found favor in the eyes of the LORD." He was a "righteous man, blameless among the people of his time, and he *walked with God*." When God saw that "all the people on earth had corrupted their ways," He found in Noah a man who would "do everything exactly as God commanded him" (Genesis 6:8-9, 12, 22). Noah was the only man on earth who chose walking with God over independence from Him. When God decided to wipe the earth clean from evil and start over with one man, Noah was His choice.

Ten more generations passed. Again, the earth was full of depravity, rebellion, and idolatry. For a second time God decided to start over with one man. In keeping with His earlier promise, He refrained from sending another flood. Instead, God selected Abram to produce a new nation of people who were to be dedicated to Him and His ways. They were to exist side by side with the pagan nations, but they were not to become like them. The influence was to work in the other direction—all nations on the earth were to be blessed through *them*. Like Noah, Abram was a "reboot" for the human race. And like Enoch, he walked with God.

Three men. That's all God had to work with, really, for *thirteen whole generations.* No wonder these "candles in the darkness" are regarded as heroes of faith to this very day (Hebrews 11:5-9).

But notice something about them: not one of the three was "religious," as we define the term. They had no special holy places; they simply walked with God. Whenever they encountered Him in some exceptional way, they might stop and build an altar to offer Him a sacrifice. But then they moved on. There was no "attending" or "revisiting" the altar. What's more, they had no religious calendars or designated holy days, as far as we know. Every day fit into a life of worship and obedience. And they had no priests or holy men standing between them and God. The lone exception is Abraham's brief encounter with the mysterious Melchizedek, the king of Salem and priest of God Most High, who blessed him and gave him bread and wine. But that was a single, unexpected meeting. There is no record of Abraham, "the friend of God," using the services of a priest at any other time in his long life.

On the whole, these three shining lights had a relationship with God remarkably *outside* the religious norm of holy place, holy time, and holy man. They were doing their best to live a "Garden of Eden" life in a tragically fallen world.

The Perfect Religion

But God had a plan. Three men were not enough to satisfy His intent for creation. That's why He had told His friend Abraham, "Look up into the sky and count the stars if you can. That's how many descendants you will have!" And He had added:

> You can be sure that your descendants will be strangers in a foreign land, where they will be oppressed as slaves for 400 years. But I will punish the nation that enslaves them, and in the end they will come away with great wealth…After four generations your descendants will return. (Genesis 15:13-14,16)

That is exactly how it worked out, of course. After four centuries, Abraham's descendents had grown into a huge nation. Through Moses and Aaron, God delivered them from their oppression. He marched them through a stormy sea and over a burning desert towards the Promised Land. Then He had them stop at a mountain so that He could do something very surprising.

God gave them a religion.

Up until then, God had stayed out of the religion business. While most of mankind had been devotedly worshiping their idolatrous impersonations of Him, bowing down in their "holy" buildings on their "holy" days with "holy" men leading them in the approved rituals, God had simply looked on in silence. He was satisfied, it seemed, with a few simple, down-to-earth men who were brave enough and humble enough to be His friends. Had that all changed?

Not really. For His own purposes, God now chose to work within fallen humanity's frame of reference by giving them the *perfect* religion and challenging a people to approach Him that way. His religion took the special place-time-man pattern to a radically higher level.

Holy place. During the Israelites' wanderings in the desert, God ordered them to construct a special holy tent. Later, after the nation had established itself in the Promised Land, God selected a city, Jerusalem, for a more permanent structure.

The basic plan was the same for both the tent and the temple. Both were rectangular structures divided by a curtain into two rooms. The larger space was called, appropriately enough, the Holy Place. In it were three pieces of furniture set aside for God's use: a lampstand with seven branches, a table for daily offerings of special bread, and an altar for burning incense to God. Behind the curtain was an even more sacred compartment, the Most Holy Place. In it was only one object: a gold-covered box signifying God's presence and His agreement, or "covenant," with the Israelites.

It is hard to overestimate the importance of the tabernacle—and later, the temple—to "God's perfect religion." The structure was the *only* approved place for the Israelites to offer their sacrifices to God. It was the required destination for faithful Israelites during the three special festival weeks. Most importantly, it represented the physical location for the presence of an infinite God among His people.

Holy times. God's calendar set aside special days, weeks, and years, each one of them rich with meaning. Every month, when the night skies announced that the moon was beginning its cycle again, they held a "new moon festival." Special sacrifices, including a sin offering, marked the observance. Each week concluded with another holy day, the Sabbath. It had been on the seventh day that God rested from His work of creation; it was on the seventh day that each Israelite was to rest from his or her work, too. Servants, slaves, even oxen and donkeys were to enjoy a break from their labors.

Then there were three special weeks every year. The Passover, held each spring, commemorated God's deliverance of Israel from slavery. It culminated in each household with a feast featuring a roasted lamb, reminding the Israelites of a very special sacrifice that had quite literally saved their lives when they were delivered from slavery. As spring ripened into summer, the Feast of Weeks was observed. It marked the time when God gave His religion to the Israelites and also celebrated the early grain harvest each year. During the autumn of the year came the special Day of Atonement, centering on the themes of repentance and sacrifice. It was followed by the week-long Feast of Booths, during which the Israelites were to "camp" in temporary huts to commemorate the forty years in which God had cared for their ancestors' needs in the desert.

Finally there were entire *years* that were designated as especially holy. Each seventh year was itself a Sabbath. The Israelites were to allow their fields and vineyards to rest from *their* work and eat only what the land produced on its own. And each fiftieth year was declared to be a year of Jubilee. All debts were canceled. All property reverted to its original owner. All slaves were set free.

There is much more we could say about the special times set aside in God's religion. But it should be obvious, at least, that the Israelites had continual opportunities to contemplate the deep things of God and to thank Him for His history of kindness towards their people.

Holy man. Israel was to be a holy nation. But within Israel there was a certain holy tribe, the descendents of Abraham's great-grandson, Levi. God chose the Levites for His service as representatives of the entire nation. During the days of the tabernacle, the Levites and *only* the Levites were allowed to touch or move the tent and its furnishings. If anyone else even approached the holy things, he or she was to be put to death. After the temple was built, the Levites were placed in charge of its work. Some prepared the holy bread; others led special songs and praises. Regardless, service to God was their life.

Within the Levite tribe was an even more select group, the descendants of Moses' brother, Aaron. They and only they could serve as priests. It was their job to offer all sacrifices and offerings to God on behalf of the nation. The priests stood in the place of the entire nation through all of the required ritual.

Finally, there was within the priestly family the most select holy man of all—the High Priest. He was the *only* human being allowed behind the curtain into the Most Holy Place, and he only went there once a year—on the Day of Atonement. Waving a smoking censer of incense, the priest sprinkled blood in front of the gold-covered box, the "Ark of the Covenant." Through this act he secured forgiveness, first for his own sin and then for the sin of the entire nation.

We could go on for hours describing the intricacy and beauty of "God's perfect religion." Nothing was without meaning, from the furnishings of the temple to the tassels on the priest's robe. God had truly taken religion—with its holy places, times, and men—to a level unequaled before or since. Over the centuries since the fall, very few men had walked with Him. But God had found a way to reveal to man deep insights into His character and mind through His religion.

Would it make a difference? Would man even care?

A Hard Lesson

How did the Jews do with this God-given religion? What was their experience, their testimony? It was a crucial test, not only for the Jews, but for us. If people are given a perfect religion, can they successfully approach God through it?

God's religion was in effect for roughly thirteen centuries between Moses and Jesus. During that entire period, we can only find a *very* few who transcended both their environment and their limitations and drew near to God through faith. Phinehas, Samuel, David, Elijah, Elisha, and a handful of other kings and prophets lived their lives with a faith that still stirs us today (Hebrews 11). All of them did their best to obey God's laws and follow the commands of His religion.

But even for these men and women, was it really the *religion* that drew them close? David, though he loved the law, learned more of God's faithfulness on the lonely hillsides of Bethlehem than he ever did by attending a Sabbath service (1 Samuel 17:34-37). Phinehas, though a priest, atoned for more sins with a spear then he ever did with a burnt offering (Numbers 25:1-13). And Elijah's most powerful sacrifice was offered on a mountain in Samaria, not in a temple in Jerusalem (1 Kings 18:30-39). Still, it is true that a few did find God within the scope of His religion during those long years.

But it is also true that the huge majority failed catastrophically.

What of God's holy place? Solomon constructed a magnificent one, the Jerusalem temple. But in spite of its beauty and deep significance to their faith, most Israelites ignored it, or worse.

In blatant disobedience to God's command that sacrifices were only to be offered at the temple, most people continued to offer them at their own shrines. The phrase, "the high places, however, were not removed; the people continued to offer sacrifices and burn incense there," appears in the records of *five different* kings of Judah. And those were the *good* kings! Sometimes the worship of pagan gods was mingled with the worship of Yahweh in those "high places." The temple, stripped of its gold and bronze repeatedly to pay off foreign kings and invading armies, eventually became as decrepit as an abandoned warehouse or a closed-down factory. One of the latter kings of Judah, Manasseh, erected altars to foreign idols in the temple itself and even sacrificed his own son on one of them. No wonder God allowed the Babylonians to burn the temple to the ground.

What of God's holy days and weeks and years? The Israelites began breaking the Sabbath almost as soon as God declared it holy (Numbers 15:32-36). They forgot to observe the Passover celebration—with all its rich meaning—from the moment they entered the Promised Land. It wasn't celebrated again until the reign of Josiah, the *twentieth* of Judah's twenty-four kings. And the year of Jubilee? As far as we know, the Israelites *never* observed it. In 1300 years, they had 26 opportunities, but missed them all.

And what of God's holy men, the priests and Levites? They were to be a special tribe within Israel—and a special family within that tribe—chosen to represent the entire nation to God. But when the kingdom split early in Israel's history, the first ruler of the northern kingdom, Jeroboam, changed all that. He wanted to give the Jerusalem temple, located in the southern kingdom, some competition, in hopes that his people would stop traveling south for the feasts and holidays. So Jeroboam fabricated two golden calves and set them up in two cities in the north. Then he "built shrines on high places and appointed priests from all sorts of people, even though they were not Levites" (1 Kings 12:31). This counterfeit priesthood and its imitation ritual was abhorrent to God (1 Kings 13).

In the kingdom of Judah, the "special men" were still the Levites, as God had commanded. But the spiritual condition of these men was scarcely better than their northern counterparts. As God Himself said, "The priests did not ask, 'Where is the LORD?' Those who deal with the law did not know Me; the leaders rebelled against Me. The prophets prophesied by Baal, following worthless idols" (Jeremiah 2:8).

These priests had the right genetics, perhaps, but not the right heart.

Again God rebuked them: "A horrible and shocking thing has happened in the land: The prophets prophesy lies, the priests rule by their own authority, and my people love it this way" (Jeremiah 5:30-31). And again: "From the least to the greatest, all are greedy for gain; prophets and priests alike, all practice deceit. They dress the wound of my people as though it were not serious. 'Peace, peace,' they say, when there is no peace" (Jeremiah 6:13-14).

The religious failure of Israel was a devastating catastrophe, far exceeding in the spiritual realm the damage from any natural disaster in the physical realm. Despite a beautiful and deeply meaningful system of holy times, places, and people, Israel as a nation utterly failed to draw near to God in faith.

Would you have done any better? Would I?

God's religion didn't fail; fallen humanity failed, and in so doing proved forever that holy place-time-man religion would *never* succeed. If God's perfect religion wasn't enough, what makes us think that *any* religion could be?

So what was God doing? Why had He even bothered instituting His religion at all? There are at least two reasons.

God's first objective was to teach man a lesson. Since the Garden, humans had wanted to believe that they were capable of choosing between good and evil. They wanted to think of themselves as capable, smart, and moral. God knew otherwise. To help our species get that point, God decided to give us an objective standard to judge ourselves by.

As Paul put it, "I would not have known what sin was except through the law…In order that sin might be recognized as sin, it produced death in me through what was good, so that through the commandment sin might become utterly sinful" (Romans 7:7,12). God wanted honest people to admit to themselves that they could never be "good." He wanted them to understand that they would never be able to approach Him through rule-keeping and rituals. *He wanted to make them desperate for another way.*

God's second objective was also to educate man, but in a more positive sense. God had placed a "subliminal message" within His religion. The details of the special times, special places, and special people foreshadowed something Higher, Truer, more Real. His "perfect religion" was merely a shadow, but there was a Reality coming. The fulfillment of so much, from the Passover lamb to the Sabbath rest, was just around the corner. The promise of a new covenant shone like a beacon lighting the way to a better future.

A New Beginning

Israel was in shambles. In a short time, the temple—what was left of it—would be burned to the ground by the invading Babylonians. The sacrifices and holidays and feasts would come to a screeching halt. The priests and prophets would be marched under guard to settle in a foreign country—if they survived the invasion at all.

Right at this moment, just when it seemed that His religion was at its lowest ebb, God breathed out a promise. It was as if a fresh, fragrant breeze blew out of Eden for just a moment, ruffling man's hair and reminding him of what he had lost—*and what he might actually regain.*

> "The time is coming," declares the LORD, "when I will make a new covenant with the house of Israel and with the house of Judah. It will not be like the covenant I made with their forefathers when I took them by the hand to lead them out of Egypt, because they broke My covenant, though I was a husband to them," declares the LORD. "This is the covenant I will make with the house of Israel after that time," declares the LORD. "I will put My law in their minds and write it on their hearts. I will be their God, and they will be My people. No longer will a man teach his neighbor, or a man his brother, saying, 'Know the LORD,' because they will all know Me, from the least of them to the greatest," declares the LORD. "For I will

forgive their wickedness and will remember their sins no more." (Jeremiah 31:31-34)

God was willing to make a new beginning. The Israelites stayed in exile for 70 years, allowing the land to catch up on the Sabbath rests it had missed over the centuries. Finally God allowed them to return, rebuild the temple, and start up their religious observances again. But God was waiting patiently until just the right moment to make His promised *new* covenant with mankind. This time, He wouldn't entrust the job to a go-between. He wouldn't use a prophet or priest—or even an angel.

This time, God would show up in Person and do the job *Himself.*

3

PARADISE REGAINED: LIFE WITH JESUS!

Imagine Once Again

Imagine walking with God. Literally…

It's evening in Palestine. The warmth of the afternoon still shimmers over the rocky hills in front of you, but behind you a cool, clean breeze stirs over the deep blue waters of Lake Galilee. The sun, riding low in the sky, bathes the landscape in gold. Soon it will paint a masterpiece over the western heights. Your senses take in the beauty. Though the lake has provided the backdrop for every scene your whole life, you never take its beauty for granted. Yet the loveliness of this summer evening cannot explain the joyful expectancy that wells up like a song inside you. There is another reason for it.

He is coming. Jesus!

He has promised that He will take you and the rest of His closest followers away for a few days. He has dismissed the crowd, that cross-section of humanity—the orthodox rule-keepers and the notorious sinners, the fanatical zealots and the traitorous tax collectors, the influential leaders and the impoverished widows. They have gone on their way, at least for a few days. Jesus is joining you now. You and your friends will hike with Him a few miles and then camp for the night. Tomorrow morning you will leave for the south, traveling down the dusty roads towards Judea and Jerusalem.

As you walk along the way, He will show you many things—birds in the sky, flowers in the field, a city set on a hill—all the while opening your mind to the wonders of God's Kingdom. You've seen birds and flowers and cities before, but never through *Jesus'* eyes. Each moment with your Friend is tinged with discovery and wonder. But the greatest joy of all is simply *to be with Him.* You call Him Teacher, but He calls you His friend. That simple fact thrills your heart!

In very many ways, Jesus seems like "one of the guys," like you. Yet at the same time, to your constant amazement, He is also very different. His words are simple, but penetrating. He avoids the complex arguments and theological hairsplitting of the rabbis. Even children love to hear Him. And when He speaks, things *happen.* The blind see. The sick are healed. The demons shriek and flee. Sometimes the dead are even raised. Those who love God walk away refreshed with joy and hope. The religious pretenders may leave feeling frustrated or angry or remorseful, but they never walk away *unchanged.*

It isn't just Jesus' words that impress you—it's *Him.* What a blend of simplicity and depth, compassion and courage, gentleness and power. And love…don't forget love! It isn't that He's gushy with emotion, though He's certainly not afraid to laugh or cry. It's that His eyes seem always focused on others rather than Himself. He genuinely cares about *who they are* and does what He can to give something real to them.

When you first met Jesus, you felt guilty about your sin and honestly a little frightened of Him. You would have been ashamed to admit it, but until then you had always found religious matters a bit dull and boring. Yet the *life* that was in this man—it is doubtful that anyone could have explained it to you, even if they had tried. When you first experienced it for yourself, it was frankly intimidating. Oh, you knew how to be religious. You could "say a prayer" or sing a Psalm in the synagogue. But Jesus seemed to chase away the comfortable familiarity and safety of religion with a single glance. It was as if He had pulled a veil away and forced you to confront God face to face. Now, *that* was terrifying at first! Once you decided to deal honestly with God about your sin, though, that feeling of being with God right *here*, right *now* was absolutely exhilarating!

Since then you have been quite literally walking with Jesus seven days a week along with a group of people that has grown closer to you than…you were about to say "family" until you suddenly remembered some of them are a part of your biological family. But I guess that proves your point!

Does that picture of life sound good to you? It should.

You were created for it.

God with Us

Mankind had failed utterly. They had failed at being their own gods; they had failed at following a perfect religion. Maybe at least some of them were ready now—ready to go all the way back to their proper place, the place they had rejected in the Garden. Maybe at least a few were ready to spit out the forbidden fruit from the Tree of the Knowledge of Good and Evil. Maybe they were ready to walk with God again. Maybe they were even ready to eat from the Tree of Life.

The moment had come for God to sign the human race up for a new agreement. Mankind needed to know the terms of it. This time, God didn't just send word through a messenger. He didn't even just bring the word Himself. This time He *was* the Word. He invaded planet earth, took on human flesh, and lived out the Word in front of us all.

Man had tried to become a god and so had lost Eden. Now God became man and offered Eden back again. For the first time in millennia, man could walk with God *literally*.

As one of Jesus' first followers said: "All this took place to fulfill what the Lord had said through the prophet: 'The virgin will be with child and will give birth to a son, and they will call him Immanuel'—which means, 'God with us'" (Matthew 1:22-23).

And as another put it:

> We proclaim to you the One who existed from the beginning, whom we have heard and seen. We saw Him with our own eyes and touched Him with our own hands. He is the Word of life. This One who is life itself was revealed to us, and we have seen Him. And now we testify and proclaim to you that He is the One who is eternal life. He was with the Father, and then He was revealed to us. We proclaim to you what we ourselves have actually seen and heard. (1 John 1:1-3)

Immanuel, "God with us," had walked on our planet for thirty quiet years. He was now ready to step out in the public view for three years more.

Religion was in for a big shock.

An Inner Kingdom

Jesus was many things—*very* many things—but a rebel was not one of them. He was, of course, born a Jew, a member of God's chosen people and a follower of God's perfect religion. Actually, He was the *only* one who ever followed the perfect religion perfectly. For that reason He grew up making pilgrimages to the temple on holy days and listening to the designated teachers (Luke 2:41-52).

When the time came for Him to start the work God had sent Him to earth to accomplish, Jesus naturally kept visiting the local synagogues and the Jerusalem temple. After all, He had been sent first and foremost to "the lost sheep of Israel," and that's where those sheep habitually gathered to hear about the things of God.

But it didn't take long before Jesus began getting Himself in trouble just about every time He set His foot in one of Israel's "holy places."

It started when He went back home to Nazareth and was invited to speak in their synagogue. The scripture reading, from the book of Isaiah, seemed to go well. But His comments afterwards were highly offensive. Jesus only managed a few sentences before the whole assembly actually attempted to murder Him!

Angry rejection—and worse—were also on the minds of some very "good, moral people" who heard Jesus speak in other synagogues (Mark 3:1-6) and in the temple itself (John 7:24-44; John 8). Before long the authorities decided to take a stand against Him: anyone who acknowledged a faith in Jesus was to be turned away at the door of the synagogue (John 9:22).

Surely this was a major blow to Jesus—to be shut out of Israel's "special places," the foundation of her religion!

The fascinating answer is *no*. It became increasingly clear: what Jesus came to accomplish had nothing to do with designated "special places" at all!

Life for Jesus and His followers took place *everywhere*. Some of His most powerful teachings occurred in the most "non-religious" settings: sitting in a fishing boat (Mark 4:1); walking through a grain field (Mark 2:23-28); relaxing at a dinner table (Luke 7:36-50); resting on a mountainside (Matthew 5:1); waiting at a well (John 4).

That's because Jesus' training of His followers was *relationship*-oriented, not *attendance*-oriented. When He met His first two followers, they asked Him, "Rabbi, where are you staying?" In response, Jesus offered friendship, not information: "Come and see!" We are told that "they went and saw where he was staying, and spent that day with him" (John 1:35-39).

With all of His disciples, Jesus emphasized relationship. The truths of Jesus were more *caught* than *taught*. "He appointed twelve—designating them apostles—that they might be with Him" first. Only after that would He send them out to proclaim God's new agreement and perform miracles to back up the message (Mark 3:14). What God had encouraged the Israelites to do with their children, He now did with His. He talked with them about God's commands when He sat at home, when He walked along the road, when He lay down, and when He got up (Deuteronomy 6:6).

Jesus had a strikingly different approach to the things of God, including "holy places," and it left Him vulnerable to attack. At His trial, Jesus' accusers claimed they had heard Him say, "I will destroy this man-made temple and in three days will build another, not made by man" (Mark 14:58, 15:29). But they missed His point, of course. Jesus had said something like that, but He was predicting His resurrection. He really wasn't interested in destroying real estate. But Jesus certainly *did* intend to change the whole concept of "temples" and "holy places" forever.

Jesus announced those intentions to the Samaritan woman. She had asked Him to solve a religious argument: "Our fathers worshiped on this mountain, but you Jews claim that the place where we must worship is in Jerusalem"—at the temple. In reply, Jesus offered this stunner: "Believe me, woman, a time is coming when you will worship the Father neither on this mountain nor in Jerusalem…a time is coming and has now come when the true worshipers will worship the Father in spirit and truth, for they are the kind of worshipers the Father seeks" (John 4:20-23).

In other words, Jesus was saying that from that point on, a worshiper's *geographical* location wasn't important. What mattered was the *spiritual* location of the worship. Was it *in* spirit and *in* truth? Implied in Jesus' statement is that the holy place for His disciples—the Garden where they could fellowship with God—was in some sense *inside people* rather than inside a building.

Jesus spelled out His intentions even more clearly when He was speaking to some of Israel's religious leaders: "Once, having been asked by the Pharisees when the kingdom of God would come, Jesus replied, 'The kingdom of God does not come with your careful observation, nor will people say, "Here it is," or "There it is," because the kingdom of God is within you'" (Luke 17:20-21).

The Kingdom that Jesus came to establish simply cannot be located geographically at all. When it is authentic, no one will even be able to point to a certain "holy place" and say that the Kingdom of God is located *there*. His Kingdom is found within a holy people. God's temple, Jesus is saying, is no longer to be built from gold, silver, and stones. God's presence is to dwell inside a temple built from *human beings*.

In that light, two of Jesus' promises take on new meaning: "For where two or three come together in my name, there am I with them" (Matthew 18:20), and "Surely I am with you always, to the very end of the age" (Matthew 28:20). Jesus really *is* Immanuel, "God with us"!

A Daily Cross

We repeat: Jesus was anything but a rebel. But He was also anything but a slave to demands, expectations, or bullying. He followed His Fathers' agenda—period. Jesus' freedom to obey the Father was nowhere more obvious than in His attitude towards *time*.

That didn't stop people from *trying* to control Jesus' schedule. Twice, Jesus responded to pressure with a gentle but firm, "My time has not yet come." And twice more, Jesus avoided capture or arrest, causing the gospel writer to comment, "His time had not yet come" (John 2:4, 7:6, 7:30, 8:20). It was clear: Jesus was going to proceed with a steady pace towards a definite goal, and no amount of manipulation would get Him off track.

Intimidation certainly wasn't going to work on Jesus, either. "Some Pharisees came to Jesus and said to him, 'Leave this place and go somewhere else. Herod wants to kill you.' He replied, 'Go tell that fox, "I will drive out demons and heal people today and tomorrow, and on the third day I will reach my goal"'" (Luke 13:31-32).

The pressure of expectations also wasn't going to move Him. When Jesus heard of His friend Lazarus' critical illness and his sisters' urgent pleas for Him to come quickly, He waited. It was a decision that would earn Him sharp criticism (John 11:37). But since Jesus' priorities required him to delay, that's exactly what He did: "When Jesus heard about it He said, 'Lazarus's sickness will not end in death. No, it happened for the glory of God so that the Son of God will receive glory from this.' So although Jesus loved Martha, Mary, and Lazarus, He stayed where He was for the next two days" (John 11:4-7). It was only *after* Lazarus died that Jesus went to him.

It's not that Jesus was selfish with His time—far from it. On more than one occasion He became so busy helping people that He didn't even have time to eat (Mark 3:20, 6:31). Even when He desperately needed rest, He kept on giving (Mark 6:32-44). Jesus was simply living His life the way He taught us to live ours—with clear priorities, with a calm heart, and with an intense focus on the current moment (Matthew 6:25-34).

That attitude towards time brought Jesus into sharp conflict with many of the "good, moral" people of His day, especially with their oh-so-religious view of the Sabbath. Jesus failed to show proper respect, in their opinion, for the holy-day habits, especially when He thought those traditions conflicted with God's priorities for the current moment. It infuriated them.

We read of two such episodes that happened back to back:

> At that time Jesus went through the grain fields on the Sabbath. His disciples were hungry and began to pick some heads of grain and eat them. When the Pharisees saw this, they said to Him, "Look! Your disciples are doing what is unlawful on the Sabbath."

> He answered, "Haven't you read what David did when he and his companions were hungry? He entered the house of God, and he and his companions ate the consecrated bread—which was not lawful for them to do, but only for the priests. Or haven't you read in the Law that on the Sabbath the priests in the temple desecrate the day and yet are innocent? I tell you that one greater than the temple is here. If you had known what these words mean, 'I desire mercy, not sacrifice,' you would not have condemned the innocent. For the Son of Man is Lord of the Sabbath."

> Going on from that place, He went into their synagogue, and a man with a shriveled hand was there. Looking for a reason to accuse Jesus, they asked Him, "Is it lawful to heal on the Sabbath?"
>
> He said to them, "If any of you has a sheep and it falls into a pit on the Sabbath, will you not take hold of it and lift it out? How much more valuable is a man than a sheep! Therefore it is lawful to do good on the Sabbath."
>
> Then He said to the man, "Stretch out your hand." So he stretched it out and it was completely restored, just as sound as the other. But the Pharisees went out and plotted how they might kill Jesus (Matthew 12:1-14).

Jesus' freedom from being controlled by the religious "special day" mentality was so shocking and revolutionary that it just about got Him killed. In fact, it was one of the reasons that He *was* killed.

In the same way Jesus lived His life, He also expected His disciples to live theirs. And this is a crucial point: *In all of Jesus' teachings recorded in the four gospels, not once did He ever command His disciples to observe the Sabbath as a special day.* Not once did He command them to observe *any* day of the week as more holy than the rest. In all of His teaching, there was only one day that Jesus commanded His disciples to set aside as holy. The name of that day?

Today.

Jesus' followers were to look on the calendar, and if it said "today," then they were to celebrate it as special, and they were to mark that celebration with a few simple "observances."

They were to commemorate every "today" by a simple, childlike dependence and trust on their Father: "Give us *today* our daily bread" (Matthew 6:11).

They were to observe every "today" by a quiet, peaceful focus on the priorities of the current moment: "I tell you not to worry about everyday life...Seek the Kingdom of God above all else, and live righteously, and He will give you everything you need. So don't worry about tomorrow, for tomorrow will bring its own worries. Today's trouble is enough for *today*" (Matthew 6:25, 33-34).

They were to celebrate every "today" by a decision to live for Jesus' satisfaction rather than their own: "If anyone would come after Me, he must deny himself and take up his cross *daily* and follow Me. For whoever wants to save his life will lose it, but whoever loses his life for Me will save it" (Luke 9:23-24).

For the followers of Jesus, every day was a celebration of life under God's loving care. Each day was a "special day"!

A Band of Brothers and Sisters

First "special places" had taken a hit, then "special times." What, then, of "special people"? Jesus wouldn't tamper with *that* aspect of religion, would He?

Would He ever!

It took many lessons and even more "hard knocks" to get His point across, but if Jesus insisted on anything, it was this: none of His followers was to be looked upon as occupying a position of power. None was to try to elevate Himself above His brothers.

To begin with, Jesus challenged their entire concept of religious authority.

> Jesus called them together and said, "You know that the rulers of the Gentiles lord it over them, and their high officials exercise authority over them. Not so with you. Instead, whoever wants to become great among you must be your servant, and whoever wants to be first must be your slave—just as the Son of Man did not come to be served, but to serve, and to give His life as a ransom for many." (Matthew 20:25-28)

Virtually everything His followers thought they knew about authority was wrong! All they had learned about leadership in the business world—or in the religious world—was turned upside down. Leadership had always been viewed as exerted from above;

it needed to be viewed as offered from *below*. For the disciples, service was to equal greatness, and slavery to others was to equal leadership. Jesus had lived that lesson. Now it was their turn to learn it.

That's why Jesus took the radical step of *forbidding His followers from using any and all religious titles.* If that statement doesn't shock you, you probably need to think about it a little more deeply! How often have you, personally, used a religious title with someone's name to indicate that they occupied a position as a "special person" in your religion? Have you ever called a man "Father Bob," "Pastor Jim," "Elder Jones," "Deacon Smith," "Reverend Johnson," or the like?

> But you are not to be called "Rabbi," for you have only one Master and you are all brothers. And do not call anyone on earth "father," for you have one Father, and He is in heaven. Nor are you to be called "teacher" [in the New American Standard, "leader"], for you have one Teacher, the Christ. The greatest among you will be your servant. For whoever exalts himself will be humbled, and whoever humbles himself will be exalted. (Matthew 23:8-12)

Jesus encouraged leadership, but He insisted that it be the leadership of one who was *among* his brothers and sisters as one who *served* (Luke 22:27). And He forbade any "caste distinctions" marking certain people out as "special," including religious titles. The truth was that all authority belonged to Jesus. While some might have a gift of leadership, they were still "all brothers." Anything beyond that, Jesus warned, was self-exaltation.

The "Religion" of Jesus

After three very public years, Jesus' physical life was drawing to a close. Soon, He would face humiliation, torture, and death. He had to. It was the Father's will. In a very real sense, Jesus had come to offer mankind a way back to the Garden, a fresh opportunity for friendship with the Living God. It required His blood to "reverse the curse" of man's rebellion. It took His death to remove the sin that had so tragically separated the entire species—including every member of it—from their Creator.

But Jesus hadn't gone straight from the carpenter shop to the cross. Those three intervening years had accomplished something vital. Without a hint of rebellion, Jesus had succeeded in turning the religious world upside down. His life was proof: being close to God didn't require being "religious" in the traditional sense. If you hung out with Jesus and really paid attention to what He said and did, you soon realized that He was redefining religion at its very core.

For Jesus, and therefore His followers, the "holy place" wasn't to be sought in a geographical location, but within a *people* belonging to God. The "special times" weren't to be regulated by a calendar. Instead, each day was to be infused with holiness through a radically fresh approach to life. And the "special people" weren't identified by positions or titles. Rather, every believer was uniquely treasured, a miraculous new creation. Each disciple could offer his or her love to the other believers through humble deeds of service, and each person was needed for the healthy functioning of the whole group.

Since the day that Adam and Eve left Eden, mankind had tried to appease God and satisfy their own consciences through religion. The gift of life Jesus offered to those who would receive it ran counter to every instinct of fallen humanity, including every religious tradition that they held so dear.

Some found the whole thing incomprehensible, frightening, infuriating, and downright dangerous. They wound up shouting "crucify Him" in the end.

But others—ah, others encountered Jesus and felt the breeze of Eden blow through their hair, beckoning them to a new life with God. And they entered in, without even a backward glance at what they left behind.

4

THE EARLY CHURCH: LIFE WITH JESUS, CONTINUED

Imagine Yet Again

Imagine walking with Jesus *living in His people…*

It will soon be evening in Jerusalem. The afternoon's lingering warmth mingles with the oven's heat in front of you. Behind you a cool breeze drifts through your window, bringing with it a hint of fresh air from the heights just outside the city. The sun, riding low in the sky, floods its golden light through that same window, illuminating the crowded kitchen with a radiance that perfectly matches what you are feeling inside. You appreciate the simple gifts—the fragrance of baking bread, the music of a friend's laughter, the beginnings of a perfect sunset. Yet the promise of a lovely summer evening cannot explain the joyful expectancy that wells up like a song inside you. There is another reason for it.

They are coming. The church, your family in Jesus!

Of course you have seen many of them throughout this day. Even now several women are finishing preparations for the evening meal, while a handful of men are carrying in a few pieces of simple furniture and several dining mats. But tonight the little house will be filled to overflowing with your fellow believers. And as you gather in His name, it will be as if Jesus Himself were right there with you!

There will be no script for the evening, just as no one has been "assigned" to "attend" tonight's meal. Every day is fresh and new. As the Master, Jesus, works in each life, He draws people together in a dynamic, ever-changing network of love. The time together this evening may be unrehearsed, but you are certain that it will be genuine and life-changing.

Some will talk about the challenges of the day and the Father's faithfulness through it. Some will share, with excitement and conviction, how they are applying the powerful teachings that they heard the evening before. Perhaps others will share a song that seems to fit the occasion perfectly. The church is alive with music these days—both the old psalms of David and the new expressions of praise emanating from the grateful hearts of the disciples. And there will be prayer—there is *always* prayer! It won't be a sterile formula, but a powerful conversation with a Living God. It just might shake the room!

Unlike the synagogue services you grew up attending, the time together won't have a "beginning" or an "end." The interactions of the day will join seamlessly with the intimate conversations over dinner. Those interactions in turn will flow right into the potent times afterwards when the whole group will be dialoguing, and they will keep on going in the quieter talks as the believers begin to return to their own homes.

The brothers and sisters are coming, and you can hardly wait until everyone arrives!

Through His people, Jesus will show you many things tonight—the wonders of His cross, the mysteries of His indwelling Spirit, the lessons of practical obedience and daily discipleship. The evening will be rich. But the greatest joy of all will simply be *spending the time with Him in His people*. That fact thrills your heart! It is doubtful that you could explain it at all to someone on the outside looking in—not that you haven't tried. But the uncomplicated truth is that Jesus is alive in His church, and you have the amazing privilege of walking with Him day by day!

Does that picture of life sound good to you? It should.

You were born for it—if indeed you have been born a second time!

A Turning Point

It all began with fifty utterly amazing days—first three, then forty, then seven.

First, there were the three days of despair. Their scenes are permanently burned into your memory. Midnight in the garden. Empty promises and hollow vows. Sleepy eyes. Bloody sweat. Torches. Soldiers. A kiss, then chaos. Lies, accusations, and mockery. Clubs, whips, and thorns. A tortured walk up a bleak hill. Splinters. Spikes. Blood. Blackened skies. Anguished cries. Silence. Numbness. Hiding. Doubts. Fear. More fear, and still more.

Next came the single moment, that euphoric instant when it finally hit you that Jesus was *ALIVE!* You had wanted to laugh, cry, dance for joy, and fall on your face, all at the same time. You could live an eternity and never forget that moment—and, according to Jesus, that's exactly what your future would hold!

After that came the forty days of wonder. It was a bit unsettling—you never knew when Jesus would show up, or where, or how long He would stay. But well before those six weeks were over, you were convinced beyond a shadow of a doubt that Jesus' resurrection was *real.* His conversations with you and your friends took on a new intensity and focus. It was as if He were trying to prepare you for something. Everything He had to say kept coming back to one topic: the *Kingdom of God.*

Then came another single moment. This time it wasn't euphoric, exactly—more like totally *awe-inspiring.* Jesus had given you what had sounded like marching orders to take His Kingdom life to people in every nation under heaven, instructing and helping them to line up their hearts and lives to His teachings. With the orders had come three promises. First, that the Holy Spirit would come on all of you. Second—and this seemed related to the first— that He would be with you always. And third, that He would come back for you. That last promise had actually been delivered by *angels*. Jesus Himself ascended into Heaven, where you are certain He is now seated at the Father's right hand. That is the awe-inspiring part!

Next came the week of joyful anticipation, when you and dozens of other believers did exactly what Jesus said: you waited in Jerusalem. Even though Jesus was gone, you felt no sense of loss— just that contagious joy. It was waiting, perhaps, but it flew by so quickly, and with such a depth of peace and praise.

Finally came the fiftieth day since the cross. It happened to be on the "day of first fruits," one of the yearly highlights in God's perfect religion. Because it was a feast day, Jerusalem was filled that morning with worshippers from all over the Roman world. Suddenly, all heaven broke loose! An invisible tornado of sound filled the room where you and Jesus' other friends were praying together. A split second later, a ball of fire was hovering in the middle of the group, as if an unseen altar had burst into flame. Within moments, the fire divided into dozens of individual flames, which flew out and landed on each person in your circle.

Now you were filled with the Holy Spirit, as Jesus had promised. Your loud praises, shouted in a myriad of languages none of you had studied, quickly drew an audience. Within minutes, the streets outside were overflowing with curious people. First Peter, then the rest of you, began to proclaim Jesus to them. A few listeners started to "get it." Then others did. Then others… Within hours, *three thousand* new believers had been baptized and joined your number. Astonishing!

But now what?

What do you do with three thousand new believers? They are all Jews. Do you point them back to observing "God's perfect religion," with exhortations to get it right this time? Or do you seize the moment to begin "teaching them to obey everything I have commanded you," as Jesus instructed? And if you make that choice, how do you go about it? Do you organize everyone into groups? Do you select regular times and places for people to meet? Do you put a pyramid leadership structure in place, to insure that everyone at least receives qualified teaching? Do you institute a priesthood? In short, do you create a new, improved religion, similar to the others you've known, but based around Jesus' teachings?

Or do you have the courage to live the way Jesus *did with you* instead?

The apostles had a decision to make. This decision was to be one of the turning points in the history of planet Earth.

The Christians' Holy Place: the Ekklesia!

What about a special place? Did the first century Christians build temples, shrines, synagogues, or sanctuaries? Jesus' life wasn't based on attendance; it was based on *relationship*. He had taken His relationships with the Father and His followers out of the confines of designated holy places and into the homes, highways, and marketplaces of Israel. The Pioneer of their faith, Jesus, had blazed a new trail. These early believers simply followed Him.

In the first days of the Jerusalem church, the believers sometimes made use of the temple courts, an outdoor, publicly-accessible area adjacent to the temple itself. For a while, the apostles continued to use the temple as a place both of prayer and of outreach to unbelievers in the community. But even in those days, the life of the church was centered elsewhere: "They broke bread in their homes and ate together with glad and sincere hearts, praising God and enjoying the favor of all the people" (Acts 2:46-47).

Soon, however, persecution permanently shut most Christians out of Israel's "special places." When Saul of Tarsus started his rampage, most believers left Jerusalem and the temple behind. Within a few years, the Jewish synagogues around the empire began to exclude Christians.

A new development made an even greater impact: Gentiles by the thousands started coming to faith in Jesus, first in Antioch, then in hundreds of cities spread over three continents. These new Christians had no notion or history of Jewish "special places." Even if they had, they were excluded from temple-worship in Jerusalem. In AD 70, of course, the whole question of the temple became academic. The Roman army responded to a Jewish revolt by leveling Jerusalem, including the temple—and it has never been rebuilt.

These early believers rejected the notion of building their own temples or shrines. Archaeologists tell us that the first known religiously-purposed building associated with Christianity wasn't constructed until the third century, over *two hundred years* after Jesus ascended to the Father!

The snapshots provided by the New Testament show that the early Christians, like Jesus, simply took their life with God out into the "real world." Paul, for example, could say, "I never shrank back from telling you what you needed to hear, either publicly or in your homes" (Acts 20:20). That's where you could find Christians gathered in the cities and villages of the empire—in a variety of public places and private homes.

Where, then, was the Christians' holy place? Jesus had prophesied that a day would come when geography would be irrelevant to spiritual life (Luke 17:20-21; John 4:20-23). Instead, the dwelling place of God would be within a *people*. And that's exactly how the early Christians saw themselves. The English word "church" is ambiguous and therefore misleading. It can refer to several things, most of which didn't even exist when the New Testament was written. Instead, the early Christians used the Greek word *ekklesia*, meaning "called out ones." They viewed themselves as being called out of the world and assembled into a new living organism, with Jesus Himself as their head. The temple—the special dwelling place of God—was no longer in a geographical location. It was within the *ekklesia*.

The persecutor-turned-apostle, Paul, saw and taught this truth with great passion and clarity:

> Consequently, you are no longer foreigners and aliens, but fellow citizens with God's people and members of God's household, built on the foundation of the apostles and prophets, with Christ Jesus Himself as the chief cornerstone. In Him the whole building is joined together and rises to become a holy temple in the Lord. And in Him you too are being built together to become a dwelling in which God lives by His Spirit. (Ephesians 2:19-22)

And again,

> Don't team up with those who are unbelievers. How can righteousness be a partner with wickedness? How can light live with darkness? What harmony can there be between Christ and the devil? How can a believer be a partner with an unbeliever? And what union can there be between God's temple and idols? For we are the temple of the living God. As God said:

> "I will live in them and walk among them. I will be their God, and they will be My people. Therefore, come out from among unbelievers, and separate yourselves from them, says the Lord. Don't touch their filthy things, and I will welcome you. And I will be your Father, and you will be My sons and daughters, says the Lord Almighty." (2 Corinthians 6:14-18)

Peter, who mostly focused on helping and teaching Christians from a Jewish background, agreed wholeheartedly:

> As you come to Him, the living Stone—rejected by men but chosen by God and precious to Him—you also, like living stones, are being built into a spiritual house to be a holy priesthood, offering spiritual sacrifices acceptable to God through Jesus Christ. For in Scripture it says: "See, I lay a stone in Zion, a chosen and precious cornerstone,

and the one who trusts in him will never be put to shame."
(1 Peter 2:4-6)

The early Christians were united in believing that Jesus lived among and within His people. And they not only believed it; they lived it.

The Christians' Holy Day: Today!

What, then, of special days? Did the early church choose a certain day of the week as sacred? Did they set aside certain seasons or "holy-days" as being particularly important? Did Jesus' *ekklesia* adopt an "ecclesiastical calendar"?

Again, the answer is a clear no.

Jesus, remember, had taught His followers many things, but observance of special days was not on the list. Instead, He had emphasized the holiness of *today*. This day—whatever it was called on the calendar—was the day to offer yourself to God in trusting, peaceful dependence (Matthew 6:11, 25, 33-34; Luke 3:23-24).

When Jesus left our planet to return to the Father, He urged His followers to teach every new convert to obey His instructions as well. That's exactly what they did in this matter of special days.

It was difficult for the new Christians, no doubt—especially for those coming from a background steeped in religious traditions. The apostles were patient with them. When someone regarded one day as more sacred than the rest, Paul recognized it as a symptom of "weak" faith, yet refused to cast judgment on him or her (see Romans 14). But when anyone tried to graft the observance of special days onto Christianity as a religion, Paul's tolerance came to an abrupt end. He wrote the Galatian *ekklesias*:

> Now that you know God—or rather are known by God—
> how is it that you are turning back to those weak and
> miserable principles? Do you wish to be enslaved by them
> all over again? You are observing special days and months
> and seasons and years! I fear for you, that somehow I have
> wasted my efforts on you. (Galatians 4:9-11)

Yes, you heard Paul right! He called observing special religious days a "weak and miserable" principle for getting to know God. The fact that the Galatians were doing so made Paul wonder whether his years of blood, sweat, and tears on their behalf had done them any good at all.

Paul was not alone in this stance. It is fascinating that in the first six decades of Christianity, as recorded in Acts and the apostolic letters, there are only three apparent references to the first day of the week, Sunday. Only one of those describes anything resembling a gathering of Christians. And that one was highly unusual: it began one day, kept going all night, continued the next morning, and featured Paul raising a young man from the dead! One day of this two-day gathering did happen to be a Sunday— since Paul was leaving town, never to return, on Monday.

In sixty years, that's it.

Those same books of the New Testament are *completely* silent about "Christian holidays." The date of Jesus' birth is not even recorded, and there is certainly no mention of the early Christians observing it for *centuries* afterwards. Similarly, the New Testament record is silent about the early Christians celebrating the day of Jesus' resurrection or ascension or any such occasion.

When they spoke of the old Jewish holy days and feasts at all, it was to point out that their meanings had been fulfilled in higher and better ways in Jesus. It was never to exhort others to observe those days.

The Passover? In the "perfect religion" God had given the Jews, it involved a feast with a sacrificial lamb and unleavened bread. But now? Paul said that *Jesus* was the believers' "Passover lamb." The *ekklesia* itself was the "unleavened bread," as long as they were filled with sincerity and truth rather than the "leaven" of malice and wickedness (1 Corinthians 5:6-8).

And the Sabbath? In the "perfect religion," it had commemorated the seventh day of the week, when God had rested from His work of creation. But now? The apostolic writings again give no hint that the Sabbath was to be transferred to a different day of the week.

The writer of Hebrews states that a "Sabbath rest" *does* remain for the people of God, but it is not entered into by observing a day of the week. Rather, believers enter that rest by ceasing from a reliance on keeping religious laws and instead believing in Jesus (Hebrews 4:1-11)!

Like their Pioneer, the early disciples did single out a day to be holy—*today*. For example:

> See to it, brothers, that none of you has a sinful, unbelieving heart that turns away from the living God. But encourage one another daily, as long as it is called Today, so that none of you may be hardened by sin's deceitfulness (Hebrews 3:7-13).

The most important day in the "Christian religion" is always *today*, no matter what the calendar says. One essential way to observe the "holiness" of today is by getting outside ourselves and finding a way to encourage, admonish, and inspire a brother or sister.

Daily encouragement was the watchword of the early believers throughout the first century. Of the Jerusalem church, we read:

> They devoted themselves to the apostles' teaching and to the fellowship, to the breaking of bread and to prayer. Everyone was filled with awe, and many wonders and miraculous signs were done by the apostles. All the believers were together and had everything in common. Selling their possessions and goods, they gave to anyone as he had need. *Every day* they continued to meet together in the temple courts. They broke bread in their homes and ate together with glad and sincere hearts, praising God and enjoying the favor of all the people. And the Lord added to their number daily those who were being saved. (Acts 2:42-47)

Years later, Paul could still say to the Ephesian *ekklesia*, "Remember that for three years I never stopped warning each of you *night and day* with tears" (Acts 20:31).

Jesus had taught that each day was to be infused with the simple religion of selfless consecration to and trust in a loving Father. That's how the early Christians lived with one another. In the end, picking out other "special days" was an expedient they just didn't need or desire.

The Christians' Holy Man: Jesus—and All Who Believe!

What, then, of "special men"? Did the early believers implement some version of a priesthood, as all other world religions had done—and still do? After all, the sudden influx of brand-new Christians did require some sort of leadership to take care of them, didn't it? Did the early churches designate certain Christians as leaders and give them titles, positions, and even salaries? Or did they once again choose "a path less traveled by," a seldom-used trail blazed by their Leader, Jesus?

To begin with, let us affirm that great men and women of faith—as God defines greatness, anyway—certainly strode the earth in those days. They did offer much help to the *ekklesias*. Without their gifts, and without the faith with which they exercised those gifts, there is no way the early believers could have grown the way they did.

But at the same time, let us also affirm that *in no way* did the early churches practice leadership by the priesthood model, with a professional "caste" of clergy. It just didn't happen that way.

Jesus' last marching orders to His followers included this ringing declaration: "All authority in heaven and on earth has been given to *Me*" (Matthew 28:18). The early believers knew and taught that when Jesus ascended to heaven, the Father had:

> ...seated Him at His right hand in the heavenly realms, far above all rule and authority, power and dominion, and every title that can be given, not only in the present age but also in the one to come. And God placed all things under His feet and appointed Him to be head over everything for the church. (Ephesians 1:20-22)

The absolute authority of Jesus was something that they took very, very seriously. In no way did they put up with someone diminishing or undermining that authority at all. One of the severest criticisms in scripture was John's statement about a "leader" named Diotrophes: "He loves to be first" (3 John 9). John was not at all amused, promising to come and "call attention to what he is doing." All authority belonged to *Jesus*. Human presumption was just not tolerated in the *ekklesias*.

The early believers knew and taught something else about Jesus' ascension: "When He ascended to the heights, He led a crowd of captives and gave gifts to His people" (Ephesians 4:8). They understood what had happened on that summer morning in Jerusalem, fifty amazing days after the cross. When the room was filled with a mighty wind and tongues of flame, Jesus was pouring out His Spirit on His people (Acts 2:33). He was apportioning His Spirit, with all of the marvelous facets of His amazing character, to human beings. As Paul put it:

> A spiritual gift is given to each of us so we can help each other. To one person the Spirit gives the ability to give wise advice; to another the same Spirit gives a message of special knowledge. The same Spirit gives great faith to another, and to someone else the one Spirit gives the gift of healing. He gives one person the power to perform miracles, and another the ability to prophesy. He gives someone else the ability to discern whether a message is from the Spirit of God or from another spirit. Still another person is given the ability to speak in unknown languages, while another is given the ability to interpret what is being said. It is the one and only Spirit who distributes all these gifts. He alone decides which gift each person should have. (1 Corinthians 12:7-11)

Each of these gifts was Jesus, distributing His Spirit among His brothers and sisters, empowering them to help one another as He had done. In that sense, each of these gifts was equally Jesus and therefore equally "authoritative" in its own way.

Leadership, then, was one such gift. As we have seen, it was to be expressed with authority, but never with authoritarianism. It shunned titles. It was lived out through relationship *with* people, not position *over* them. Its goal was to equip people to exercise *their* gifts, not to squelch others through control or "micromanagement."

That is why when the early *ekklesias* met together for encouragement, prayer, teaching, and worship, there is not even a hint of a "designated speaker" or "master of ceremonies" in charge. There was no division of people into "pulpit" and "pew." No one was controlling the meeting—except Jesus.

Here is the best description in the entire New Testament of how Christians were to meet:

> What then shall we say, brothers? When you come together, everyone has a hymn, or a word of instruction, a revelation, a tongue or an interpretation. All of these must be done for the strengthening of the church. If anyone speaks in a tongue, two—or at the most three—should speak, one at a time, and someone must interpret. If there is no interpreter, the speaker should keep quiet in the church and speak to himself and God. Two or three prophets should speak, and the others should weigh carefully what is said. And if a revelation comes to someone who is sitting down, the first speaker should stop. For you can all prophesy in turn so that everyone may be instructed and encouraged. (1 Corinthians 14:26-31)

How were the *ekklesias* to meet? Everyone was responsible to use his or her gifts to build up the rest. All gifts were welcomed and valued. There were many different kinds of "flowers" in the "bouquet" of Christian gatherings, and each was welcomed. No single person dominated. Each individual submitted to the others, to the point of stopping in mid-sentence if another person received a revelation from God! In this way, everyone "prophesied in turn" and so everyone was "instructed and encouraged."

For all of these reasons and more, nothing remotely resembling a "professional priesthood" or clergy arose for many, many decades of early Christian life. It was foreign to their experience of Jesus. Leadership, yes; a "clerical caste system," no.

In the matter of "special people," the early believers lived out the new agreement God had made with them through Jesus. It was vastly different from human religion, but it was the only way of life they knew:

> "This is the covenant I will make with the house of Israel after that time," declares the LORD. "I will put my law in their minds and write it on their hearts. I will be their God, and they will be my people. No longer will a man teach his neighbor, or a man his brother, saying, 'Know the LORD,' because they will all know Me, from the least of them to the greatest," declares the LORD. "For I will forgive their wickedness and will remember their sins no more." (Jeremiah 31:33-34)

The "Religion" of Christianity is the "Religion" of Jesus

What was the "church life" like in AD 30-70? It was identical, really, to the "disciples' life" during the last three years of Jesus' physical existence. That experience of intimate fellowship had simply been transplanted geographically to the cities and villages of the Roman Empire.

According to Luke, the gospel that he wrote described what Jesus "*began* to do and teach" (Acts 1:1). The book of Acts, then, was what Jesus *continued* to do and teach, *after* His ascension. This time He was "doing and teaching" through His people, the *ekklesia*.

First century believers, then, saw themselves as continuing the life that the earliest followers had enjoyed with Jesus on the hills and highways of Galilee and Judea. They were still His spiritual family, "seated in a circle around Him" (Mark 3:34). They still hung on His every word. They still built their lives on the foundation of putting those words into practice. Acts 2:42-49 is really only a description of several thousand people putting Matthew 5-7 into practice together.

The "religion" of Christianity is in truth only meant to be the "religion" of Jesus. It is nothing more—and certainly nothing less.

When they rebelled in the Garden, mankind forfeited a life of intimate, loving, face-to-face dependence on God. Religion—with its categorization of times, places, and people into "holy" and "secular"—proved to be a poor substitute for Paradise. When God offered a perfect religion, rich with meaning, the human race had proved itself incapable of living it. Jesus was God's mind-blowing answer to this dilemma. For the first time in millennia, human beings had an opportunity to walk with God face to face in loving dependence. When Jesus returned to heaven, that opportunity was not lost. Far from it! "Christ-ianity" was merely the name people gave that life of intimate reliance *after* the ascension.

The early believers proclaimed with clarity, courage, and joy that Jesus died, that He was buried, that He rose again, that He ascended to the Father's right hand, and that He poured out His Spirit on His followers. Jesus was not a dead hero or dearly beloved founder. He was *alive* and very actively involved in the lives of His people.

Christianity in those days required no religious trappings. It blew past the special time-place-man paradigm into a new Reality of relationship, both with God and with His people.

If you have been born a second time, that life is your birthright.

5

THE NEXT GENERATION: GRAVITY'S TUG

Ekklesia Life

The human species was created for one purpose: friendship with God.

Once, in a place not so far away and a time not so long ago, man and woman lived with their Creator in a state of peaceful contentment and loving submission. They experienced His love and care every second of the day and in every square foot of their paradise home. They lost their whole reason for existence, though, with a tragically stupid attempt at being their *own* gods. And it didn't work. Humans failed miserably at being independent mini-divinities.

But in an amazing display of creativity and love, God gave humanity a second chance at friendship. He began by showing up in Person and literally walking with anyone who was humble enough to appreciate the opportunity. After accomplishing His purpose through the cross, He returned to heaven. But God didn't just stay there, located in some inaccessible dimension outside our universe. Instead, He poured Himself out on every man and woman who was finally ready to enter into the loving, trusting submission that their species had rejected in the Garden.

God created a *new* paradise, a new place to walk in friendship with man. That place was known as the *ekklesia*, the church. It was built from an interwoven network of lives, linked together daily by a common devotion to Jesus and to each other.

Christianity in those days was unlike anything the world had seen since Eden. It was unheard of in history: a race of people who surrendered their autonomy and welcomed their Creator to move into the little nooks and crannies of their daily lives. No longer did they try to confine Him to a few special days or a handful of special places. No longer did they create special men as buffers to stand between them and their God. Now every day called "today" was special. Every place where the *ekklesia* set its feet, whether "in public" or "from house to house" was holy. Every member, "from the least to the greatest," was a "royal priest."

The results were nothing short of amazing.

People who once were full of hatred, selfishness, and bitterness now *loved* one another desperately. People who once were enslaved by every kind of addictive passion and pleasure now lived in glorious freedom. People who once worshipped rocks and sticks now had an intimate knowledge of the Living God.

The *ekklesia* was Paradise reestablished in the midst of a fallen world. It was "paradise" for the same reason Eden had been: men and women could find their Creator there and "walk with Him in the cool of the day." Paradise did not mean "utopia," of course. Problems happened. But the *ekklesia* provided a ground where problems could be solved. The apostles' letters to the local *ekklesias* occupying the cities of the Roman empire were full of practical instruction and direction on how to resolve the causes of any confusion or disorder. And people *listened*. Even in the weakest, most immature local assemblies, people overcame every obstacle to experiencing true Life (see, for example, 2 Corinthians 7:5-16).

The first century church soared with God on eagle's wings. But the pull of gravity never went away. The fallen world—with its pagan notions of religion and carnal values of independence and self-indulgence—never stopped tugging at the believers, trying to drag them down into fallen humanity's realm once again. For a generation or more, it was as if the *ekklesias* defied gravity. And truly, they could have kept soaring higher and higher with God if they chose to, right up until the return of Jesus. But as the century drew near a close, the New Testament bears witness that the world's gravity was starting to have an effect.

Just before AD 70, six persons of extraordinary spiritual stature—one of them with quite amazing stature—wrote letters warning of decline and urging the *ekklesias* to take their faith to a higher level than they had ever known. These letters make up eleven of the last books in our New Testament.

Paul

Paul had once been the *ekklesias'* fiercest persecutor. But after Jesus quite literally knocked him off his horse, Paul became their most devoted servant. In an astonishing turn-around, the man who once dedicated his life to crushing the *ekklesias* received the radically different assignment of establishing and strengthening new *ekklesias* throughout the Roman world.

The end of Paul's earthly existence was now drawing near. Soon he would die at the hands of a Roman executioner. First, however, he would write three letters to Timothy and Titus, brothers he considered faithful and gifted, to help them carry on with the work of the gospel. He filled these letters with notes of concern and alarm about the direction the church seemed to be drifting.

Already, a few people were abandoning the Life and freedom of the gospel for a religion tainted with human tradition and philosophy. They were wandering away from the simplicity of "love, which comes from a pure heart and a good conscience and a sincere faith" and turning instead to "meaningless talk" (1 Timothy 1:3-7). They had developed an "unhealthy interest in controversies and quarrels about words, resulting in envy, strife, malicious talk, evil suspicions and constant friction." They were now "men of corrupt mind, who had been robbed of the truth and who thought that godliness was a means to financial gain" (1 Timothy 6:3-5). In fact, a desire to make a buck from peddling God seemed to be their main motive (Titus 1:10-11). They had already "shipwrecked" their own faith and now were threatening the faith of others (1 Timothy 1:18).

These people were still a small, though troublesome, minority. But Paul could foresee a day when many others would also refuse to "put up with sound doctrine. Instead, to suit their own desires," they would "gather around them a great number of teachers to say what their itching ears" would "want to hear." They would "turn their ears away from the truth and turn aside to myths" (2 Timothy 4:3-4).

The results would be catastrophic:

> The Spirit clearly says that in later times some will abandon the faith and follow deceiving spirits and things taught by demons. Such teachings come through hypocritical liars, whose consciences have been seared as with a hot iron. They forbid people to marry and order them to abstain from certain foods, which God created to be received with thanksgiving by those who believe and who know the truth. (1 Timothy 4:1-3)

And again:

> There will be terrible times in the last days. People will be lovers of themselves, lovers of money, boastful, proud, abusive, disobedient to their parents, ungrateful, unholy, without love, unforgiving, slanderous, without self-control, brutal, not lovers of the good, treacherous, rash, conceited, lovers of pleasure rather than lovers of God—having a form of godliness but denying its power. (2 Timothy 3:4)

Paul's advice to Timothy? "Have nothing to do with them." Paul was not speaking of a "tribulation" in some distant century, but of a time he fully expected that Timothy would live to see. Remember, to the early believers, the "last days" had already begun (Acts 2:17; Hebrews 1:2; James 5:3).

How did Paul try to prepare these brothers—and through them, the church as a whole—for this coming crisis? He reminded them of the bedrock foundations of the gospel he had passed on to them. He stressed the pivotal importance of the *ekklesia*, "the pillar and foundation of the truth," and provided practical direction for teaching its members how to function as a healthy unit. He emphasized strongly in each of the letters that leadership is *recognized* by character and personal fruitfulness, not *conferred* by position or title or office. And he braced them for the strenuous work ahead with some of the most inspiring exhortations in the entire Bible.

Paul was anything but defeatist. He remained to the very end a man of vision, faith, and hope. Yet as the first generation of believers passed the baton to the second, Paul was deeply concerned. The ultimate victory of the church was secure; God *would* "crush satan under their feet." But would the next few generations be ready to overcome the evil one? Would the *ekklesia* remain a "garden" where God and man could walk in intimacy? Or was it drifting towards a distressing future?

Peter and Jude

Other men of God were pondering the same questions at the same time. Peter, like Paul, had been an awe-struck participant in some of the mightiest outpourings of God's power in his or any generation. Peter had walked on water. He had experienced the miracle of Pentecost. He had been delivered from prison by an angel. He had seen the Holy Spirit fall on gentiles. He had witnessed the dead raised—both physically and spiritually. No one had to convince Peter of God's power. He had *lived* in that power from the moment he first met Jesus. It was impossible for Peter to be a pessimist, and yet as his life drew to a close, he, too, shared Paul's deep concern that the church was heading for a crucial fork in the road.

Peter responded with a pair of open letters, addressed not to an individual or even a specific *ekklesia*, but to believers throughout the eastern half of the Roman empire. His first letter, written around AD 64, was meant to strengthen the *ekklesias* in the foundations of their faith and to stiffen their spiritual backbones in the face of persecution. But his second letter, written only a year or two later, sounded a much more urgent note of warning. Something had happened—either in Peter's environment or in his spirit—to deepen his concern for the *ekklesias'* future. He knew that he would a scant year later "put aside the tent of his body" (2 Peter 1:13-14). He had some things he just had to say before he left the planet.

Peter began this second letter with strong exhortations to the believers that they "make every effort" to "add to their faith" with a practical growth towards maturity. He challenged them to remain true to the prophecies of scripture as well as to the testimony of the apostles. But his main emphasis was a potent warning about the challenges they would soon face from counterfeit leaders, teachers, and "scoffers" who would totally misdirect the church if left unchecked:

> There will be false teachers among you. They will secretly introduce destructive heresies, even denying the sovereign Lord who bought them—bringing swift destruction on themselves. Many will follow their shameful ways and will bring the way of truth into disrepute. In their greed these teachers will exploit you with stories they have made up. Their condemnation has long been hanging over them, and their destruction has not been sleeping. (2 Peter 2:1-3)

The people who read these words were Peter's "dear friends," and he was confident that they "already knew" better than to drift into false religion. Still, he felt the pressing need to warn them: "Be on your guard so that you may not be carried away by the error of lawless men and fall from your secure position. But grow in the grace and knowledge of our Lord and Savior Jesus Christ" (2 Peter 3:17-18).

Were the *ekklesias* really in danger of being "carried away" by religious error? Could they actually "fall" from their "secure position"?

Peter wasn't the only one who thought so. Jesus' half-brother, Jude, wrote a very similar letter, probably a year or so after Peter. In fact, Jude may well have read Peter's letter and sent out his own shorter note to underscore the warnings Peter had given. Without a doubt, Jude expressed the very same concerns in similar language:

> Dear friends, although I was very eager to write to you about the salvation we share, I felt I had to write and urge you to contend for the faith that was once for all entrusted to the saints. For certain men whose condemnation was written about long ago have secretly slipped in among you. They are godless men, who change the grace of our God into a license for immorality and deny Jesus Christ our only Sovereign and Lord. (Jude 3-4)

The rest of Jude's short but powerful letter stressed his concern that his "dear friends" needed to "remember what the apostles of our Lord Jesus Christ foretold": "'In the last times there will be scoffers who will follow their own ungodly desires.' These are the men who divide you, who follow mere natural instincts and do not have the Spirit" (Jude 17-19).

Jude exhorted his readers to "build themselves up in their most holy faith" (Jude 20). God was able to "keep them from falling" (Jude 24), but the possibility of the world's gravity pulling them down from their secure position was very real.

The Writer of Hebrews

Around the same time, an anonymous author wrote still another open letter addressed to believers from a Jewish background. We call it Hebrews. We may not know the author's name, but we know for certain that he had a deep revelation of Jesus and an equally deep concern about the current state and future direction of the church. This writer, too, sensed that the tug of the world was having its effect on the *ekklesias*. "We must pay more careful attention, therefore, to what we have heard," he wrote, "so that we do not drift away. For if the message spoken by angels was binding, and every violation and disobedience received its just punishment, how shall we escape if we ignore such a great salvation?" (Hebrews 2:1-3)

It is the same feel we get from the last letters of Paul, Peter, and Jude: the church was at risk, because it was drifting away from something crucially important.

For one thing, the believers were losing their grip on the fundamental, bedrock teachings of Jesus and His apostles:

> We have much to say about this, but it is hard to explain because you are slow to learn. In fact, though by this time you ought to be teachers, you need someone to teach you the elementary truths of God's word all over again. You need milk, not solid food! Anyone who lives on milk, being still an infant, is not acquainted with the teaching about righteousness. But solid food is for the mature, who by constant use have trained themselves to distinguish good from evil. (Hebrews 5:11-14)

The writer felt compelled to give his readers strong cautions against dabbling in false teaching: "Do not be carried away by all kinds of strange teachings. It is good for our hearts to be strengthened by grace, not by ceremonial foods, which are of no value to those who eat them" (Hebrews 13:9).

The readers were also being lured by temptations to worldliness and sin. The writer of Hebrews gave them this stern warning:

> It is impossible for those who have once been enlightened, who have tasted the heavenly gift, who have shared in the Holy Spirit, who have tasted the goodness of the word of God and the powers of the coming age, if they fall away, to be brought back to repentance, because to their loss they are crucifying the Son of God all over again and subjecting Him to public disgrace. (Hebrews 6:1-4)

Such strong language! The first century believers had enjoyed a potent spiritual Life. They had "tasted the powers of the coming age." How many Christians since that day could honestly make that claim? And yet their spiritual position was far from secure.

Besides voicing a deep concern about his readers' spiritual direction, what did the Hebrews writer do to help them turn things around?

First, the writer held up Jesus, describing in towering language how He was both the sacrifice for sin and the High Priest who offered that sacrifice. The words "Jesus" and "today" appear over and over in the letter. The readers needed to understand that Jesus was ever living and continually available, that a "right here, right now" relationship with God was always possible through Him.

Next, the writer held up the vital importance of the *ekklesia* as God's fortress for defeating the evil one. If each believer lived in the *daily* encouragement and exhortation of brothers and sisters, then the attraction of sin would lose its power to deceive (Hebrews 3:12-14). Further, each member of the church was to take personal responsibility to consider how to inspire and motivate his or her fellow believers towards love and good works (Hebrews 10:24-25).

Finally, the writer exhorted his readers to look back on the heroes of faith for inspiration for the challenges ahead (Hebrews 11). They must not only hold their position but press ahead even higher: "So do not throw away your confidence; it will be richly rewarded. You need to persevere so that when you have done the will of God, you will receive what He has promised" (Hebrews 10:35-36).

The need of the hour, judging from all of these letters, was a decisive refocusing on both the Person and teachings of Jesus, an unwavering loyalty to the Life of the local *ekklesia*, a clear rejection of religious deception, and a whole-hearted commitment to moving forward in faith.

John

During his early years, John—"the apostle Jesus loved"—had enjoyed a profound friendship with his Teacher. For three years the "band of brothers and sisters" who followed Jesus had experienced "walking with God in the cool of the day." John, more than anyone, had grasped the immense privilege they had been given. He was never far from Jesus. John had been with Jesus on the Mountain of Transfiguration and with Him on the Mount of Olives. John had been one of the few to risk his life by standing near the foot of the cross. He had also been the very first apostle to believe that Jesus was raised from the dead. John, together with Peter, had been at the forefront of proclaiming the risen Christ throughout Judea and Samaria. He had been a pillar of the Jerusalem *ekklesia*.

John knew what living "right here, right now" with Jesus meant, not only when Jesus was living in His physical body, but also when He was living in His Body, the church. He understood how critically important it was for the *ekklesias* to reject the religious low road and instead press ever higher with their Lord.

That's no doubt why, as the first generation of believers gave way to the second and third, John felt so deeply concerned about what he saw. He, too, sensed a "drift." In response, he wrote three letters that are preserved in our New Testament—two short notes of warning to specific locations, and one lengthy letter sent to *ekklesias* at large. It is no coincidence that John wrote his letters at the same time Paul, Peter, and Jude were writing about their own sense of concern.

In the remarkable first letter, John laid out in clear terms a series of tests designed to distinguish genuine Christianity from mere religion. Jesus was Real. John had heard, seen, and touched Him. Fellowship with Jesus *right here, right now* could be equally Real. But it required living in the light—calling sin what it is, and coming to Jesus for forgiveness in honesty and exposure, whenever any darkness crept into the believer's life. It meant obeying Jesus in practical daily living. In fact, it meant living the way Jesus did. It demanded both unwavering love and unflinching rejection—love for brothers and sisters, and rejection of the world and its ways. It called for an eager expectation for Jesus' return and a passionate pursuit of purity in preparation for His coming.

A Real relationship with Jesus always changed a person's life, according to John. After all, Jesus had come to planet earth to "destroy the works of the devil." That's exactly what He would do when He came into a person's *life* as well.

John was determined to uphold the standard of genuine Christianity. He also wanted to warn the believers about the false religion that he could see tugging at the church. It was imperative that the *ekklesias* "not believe everyone who claimed to speak by the Spirit." Instead, they needed to "test them to see if the spirit... comes from God." For there were "many false prophets in the world" (1 John 4:1).

He urged them:

> Dear children, this is the last hour; and as you have heard that the antichrist is coming, even now many antichrists have come. This is how we know it is the last hour...See that what you have heard from the beginning remains in you. If it does, you also will remain in the Son and in the Father. And this is what He promised us—even eternal life. I am writing these things to you about those who are trying to lead you astray. As for you, the anointing you received from Him remains in you, and you do not need anyone to teach you. But as His anointing teaches you about all things and as that anointing is real, not counterfeit—just as it has taught you, remain in Him. (1 John 2:18-27)

He sounded the same note of warning in a brief letter to a specific local *ekklesia*, a writing we now call 2 John:

> Many deceivers, who do not acknowledge Jesus Christ as coming in the flesh, have gone out into the world. Any such person is the deceiver and the antichrist. Watch out that you do not lose what you have worked for, but that

> you may be rewarded fully. Anyone who runs ahead and does not continue in the teaching of Christ does not have God; whoever continues in the teaching has both the Father and the Son. If anyone comes to you and does not bring this teaching, do not take him into your house or welcome him. Anyone who welcomes him shares in his wicked work. (2 John 7-11)

There was a rumor circulating throughout the first century that John would never die but would stay on earth until Jesus' return. John knew differently. He realized just how short his remaining days were. He also realized how grave a danger the church was already facing from the gravitational pull of the world and from fleshly human religion. That is why he worked so hard to recalibrate the believers' understanding about what Christianity even *meant*. There was a real danger that something immensely precious—something John had heard, seen, and touched—could actually be forgotten in the coming generations.

Jesus Himself

The years passed. The close of the first century was rapidly approaching. Peter and Paul had long since "graduated" to a full time residence in heavenly realms. Virtually all the first generation of disciples had exited planet earth as well. John was one of the few who remained. As the elderly "disciple whom Jesus loved" was in exile on the island of Patmos, his Master decided to give him one last assignment: to write what we now call Revelation.

Jesus began His visit with John by dictating seven remarkable letters, addressed to seven local *ekklesias* in Asia Minor. They were not signed by John this time, but by Jesus Himself. These letters provide a snapshot of the "state of the church" in this entire region around AD 90. The composite picture is disquieting: five of the seven *ekklesias* receive a warning or rebuke from Jesus.

There are at least two disturbing trends. First, there was a pervasive slide towards false teaching. What the apostles had foreseen was now happening. Bogus apostles, "Nicolaitans," and "Jezebel" were trying to peddle lies as some sort of "deep secret." They were luring many into pagan notions of "mystery religion" that basically amounted to nothing more than a sloppy gratification of fleshly appetites. These false teachers were making alarming inroads into several of the *ekklesias*, and in most of them, they were being "tolerated." Jesus was not pleased.

Second, there was a creeping spiritual lethargy and dullness beginning to set in. Jesus rebuked one *ekklesia* for being dead, another for being lukewarm, and a third for forsaking its first love. The *ekklesias* had largely ignored the warnings of the apostles and prophets. They were allowing the pagan world's gravity to tug them down to its level. Something had to be done, and soon. Jesus urged them, "Remember the height from which you have fallen! Repent and do the things you did at first."

Jesus then issued an admonition that included some of the most alarming words in scripture: *"If you do not repent, I will come to you and remove your lampstand from its place"* (Revelation 2:5).

The term "lampstand" is a word picture that stood for the identity of these local assemblies of believers as *ekklesias* in the sight of God (see Revelation 1:12-20). When Jesus spoke of removing their lampstand, He was warning them that if their current spiritual decline continued, at least one of the seven churches would soon lose the right to be called an *ekklesia!* They might continue indefinitely as a religious society, but they would no longer be a genuine church. Jesus would no longer walk in friendship among them.

It would be paradise lost all over again.

It had been a remarkable century, beginning with the birth of Jesus, continuing with His life and death and resurrection, progressing with His establishment of the *ekklesia* as His home on earth, and culminating with the spread of *ekklesia*-life throughout the Roman world. During these few remarkable years, God had reversed the curse that had hung over the human race for millennia.

But what would this new race of humanity do with this precious gift? As the next century began, would they go on to soar to new heights with God? Or would they allow gravity to drag them down from their "secure position" in Jesus?

6

PARADISE FORGOTTEN: CHRISTIANITY GETS RELIGIOUS

Roman Paganism

As her legions spread out across three continents, "Rome the conqueror became the conquered." Whenever a new culture was absorbed, its practices and beliefs deeply impacted the increasingly pluralistic empire. Religion was certainly no exception. If you lived in Rome during the second and third centuries, you had a "cafeteria line" of religions to choose from. In reality, though, most of the religions were cooked from the same few ingredients. Only the "presentation" changed.

The main ingredient and underlying assumption of any pagan religion was *polytheism*. There were literally thousands of "gods" and semi-divine "heroes." Each had authority over a specific area of the natural world or human society, it was believed. Some were big, governing the ocean or the sun or the sky. Others were much more local, with a sphere of influence that might not reach past a specific river or hill. But all were considered divine, and it was thought appropriate to worship any or all of them—which is why the empire could so easily welcome new religions into the pagan mix.

There was another key assumption in paganism: the "gods" had a nasty temper, and you wouldn't like them if they got angry. They were petty, jealous, volatile, and criminally unconcerned about "collateral damage" from their tantrums. Was your city threatened by barbarian raiders? It was because the "god of war" was upset about something. Better tie up his idol with chains to restrain him! Was a plague devastating your entire region? Probably the "earth goddess" was resenting the fact that the "sun god" had killed her child a thousand years earlier. Better set up a statue of the "sun god" holding bow and arrows so that he could "shoot away" the disease. Did an earthquake damage your town, even knocking down the pillars in one of your pagan temples? Obviously the "god of quakes" was angry with that temple's "god." Better enlist a third "god" to rebuke him for you.

These illustrations are not fiction. They are actual examples from Roman history showing how people interpreted crises. And they demonstrate two other core beliefs of paganism.

First, *human suffering wasn't caused by human sin, but by "divine" sin.* In Greek and Roman myths, the "gods" and "heroes" committed acts of murder, infanticide, immorality, deception, and betrayal. Their unpredictable anger at humans or at each other was the true source of human misery. And second, *the important thing in religion was to appease the "gods" with the proper ritual performed at the proper place and time.* Personal holiness in thought and conduct, twenty-four hours a day and seven days a week, really wasn't necessary. The "gods" didn't really care if your thoughts were free from greed or lust as you walked through the marketplace. They were much more concerned with getting your respect as you passed by their shrines. Religion, then, was a lot like office politics: it was about knowing how to keep a bad-tempered boss—who could either make you or break you—on your side.

In a typical Roman city, you could worship at the pagan "denomination" of your choice, with a variety of temples and shrines dedicated to various "gods." The temple would have an idol of some sort and an altar, housed in an ornate structure. In practical terms, appeasing the "gods" meant keeping their idols clean and tidy, offering them daily animal sacrifices, and honoring them with special festivals. Once a year, perhaps, the idol would be taken out on a parade around the city, led by special "worship teams" of musicians, singers, and dancers.

Temples or shrines were also a place where you might go for religious advice. At some, you could throw dice or choose letters of the alphabet, which would let you pick from a list of general answers, which read something like fortune cookies in a Chinese restaurant. Other shrines had much more elaborate oracles. Cities hundreds of miles away might send whole delegations, complete with choirboys, to the oracle to ask how to avert a plague or end a famine. Individuals also might make the pilgrimage to inquire about their future prospects or to settle their philosophical questions. These shrines combined the concept of "special place" and "special men." A typical oracle required the services of a "priest" to perform sacrifices, a "prophet" to groan and mutter incoherently, and a "thespode" to interpret these noises of alleged inspiration and phrase them in a verse or two of Greek poetry for the paying customers.

God, then, was viewed as neither friendly nor accessible nor immediate. He was—or in the pagan view, "they were"—*almost* safely confined in the "box" provided by religion. Roman paganism illustrates clearly what happened to human society after the Fall. Humanity felt in its heart its separation from God. Human beings could not deny God's existence or their own need for His favor for survival on a fallen planet. Still, humans craved as much independence from God as they could get. The solution was religion. The citizens of the empire attached the notion of "god" to certain special places and times and to rituals conducted by trained specialists. By attending to this religion, they hoped to avoid divine anger and attain divine blessing for their crops and families and towns. This external religion "freed" them from needing to worry about personal sin or submission to God on any intimate daily basis.

The pagan twist on theology explains why they so hated the early Christians: these followers of the crucified carpenter were "atheists" who refused to honor the "gods" with ritualistic worship. By being so stubborn, the Christians were inviting disaster. No one cared what they believed; the empire was willing to absorb another religion. But their rejection of tradition and their refusal to make even a token offering of incense was viewed as a threat to society. Earthquake, famine, plague, and war could at any moment decimate the most cultured and technologically advanced empire the world had ever seen. If it happened, it would be because the Christians had insulted the "gods."

Respect was the *last* thing the early Christians felt for paganism, however. The Christians weren't really "atheists" when it came to the "gods" of Rome. They rejected the notion that an idol could be a "god," but they accepted that there was nevertheless some sort of spiritual power at work in the pagan religions. As Paul wrote, "My dear friends, flee from idolatry…Do I mean then that a sacrifice offered to an idol is anything, or that an idol is anything? No, but the sacrifices of pagans are offered to demons, not to God, and I do not want you to be participants with demons" (1 Corinthians 10:14, 19-20).

Yes, you heard right: Paul called the Roman "gods" *demons*, and this language was no more politically correct in the pluralistic Roman empire of the first century than it would be in the pluralistic western world of our own day. Christian writers and teachers of the second and third centuries agreed with Paul. In their disputes with pagans, they did not try to deny stories of miracles associated with particular shrines or idols. They did, however, attribute those miracles to the power of demons. Pagan religions did not include the concept of a satan or devil, but the Christians countered that *all* of pagan worship was directed towards the "spiritual forces of evil in heavenly realms."

During these centuries, then, the Christians were a small minority "in, but not of" a hostile world. They were threatened within and without: within, by the "gravitational attraction" of human flesh for human religion, and without, by the pressure of an antagonistic pagan majority.

"Going to Church" with the New Generation

We should certainly not think that the believers during this period lowered their standards and happily blended in with paganism. Quite the opposite is true; they actually went to great lengths to remain separate. Christians visiting or relocating to a community were not welcomed into assemblies without at least one good letter of recommendation and a vote of confidence from at least one member. During gatherings, many churches posted guards at the door to discourage unattested people from entering. These practices were common not only during times of persecution, but in times of peace, earning Christians the label "exclusive" from their derisive pagan neighbors.

Conversion to the faith *never* took place by a pagan deciding to "go to church," where he heard a good "sermon" and an "altar call," and then responded by praying with a "counselor." These modern practices were entirely unknown during the second and third centuries. Instead, conversion was a rigorous three-year apprenticeship, during which the candidate was told to stop sinning and was watched closely for any lapses in behavior. Apprentices received teaching in the basics of the faith but were not allowed to meet with the church, to take the Lord's Supper, or even to receive baptism until the three-year trial was over.[1]

It's safe to say, then, that Christians during this era remained loyal to the *concept* of being a "holy nation" and a "separate people." But what of the warnings of the apostles and prophets—and of Jesus Himself—that brought the New Testament revelation to a close? Did the "terrible times" they envisioned come to pass? One way to answer that question is to look for the hallmarks of human religion. Did these Christians drift from an interwoven life of simple submission and trust? Did they instead start compartmentalizing life and designating certain places, times, or people as "special" and the rest, by implication, as "common"?

In the matter of "holy places," the answer appears to be "no." We are certain of this: there were no "church buildings" erected on public grounds until the end of the third century—*none at all.* Christians continued to meet primarily in homes. The only hints that spiritual life was starting to become "located" in special places came near the end of this period, when well-to-do Christians began remodeling their houses to accommodate larger gatherings. Archaeologists tell us that in the town of Duro-Europos, near the Euphrates, Christians began meeting in a private home with a room that could hold around thirty people. Sometime around the year 240, the owner of the house did some remodeling, knocking down a wall to create a larger room that could accommodate sixty. A tub was also installed around this time, presumably for use in baptisms. But this structure remained a private home. It was not a "sanctuary" or "church building," let alone a cathedral. There is no suggestion, either from archaeology or in the numerous early Christian writings that such structures existed for over two centuries after Pentecost.

When it comes to "special times," however, we do find *significant* evidence that "the faith that was given the holy people of God once and for all time" was steadily morphing into something quite different. For the earliest Christians, remember, the "holy day" was *any* day called "today." But by the mid-second century, we read the earliest known reference to Sunday as a special day for Christians. It comes from the pen of Justin, a converted pagan philosopher who taught theology in Rome.

> But Sunday is the day on which we all hold our common assembly, because it is the first day on which God, having wrought a change in the darkness and matter, made the world; and Jesus Christ our Savior on the same day rose from the dead. For He was crucified on the day before that of Saturn (Saturday); and on the day after that of Saturn, which is the day of the Sun, He rose. (Justin Martyr, *The First Apology,* Chapter 67)

It took five generations after Pentecost. But in Rome, at least, a "Christian holy day" had been born, and with it a twin known as the "Sunday service." It was a development of historic importance. Christianity had always been focused on relationship, not meetings. Change was on the way.

A third-century work from Syria called the "Didascalia" gave rules for the worship service. There was to be assigned seating or standing room for specific ages and genders. A reader was to stand "upon some high place" and present two selections from the Old Testament. Then a soloist was to sing some Psalms, with the people "joining at the conclusion of the verses." The singing was followed by readings from the New Testament. The congregation then was to rise, face the east, and pray. After the members greeted one another with a kiss, they were to come forward "by ranks" to partake of the bread and wine. Apparently the service was not expected to be too exciting; a deacon was appointed to "oversee the people, that nobody may whisper, nor slumber, nor laugh, nor nod; for all ought in the church to stand wisely, and soberly, and attentively, having their attention fixed upon the word of the Lord."

Contrast that description with the only instruction in the *entire New Testament* about how Christians should handle their corporate gatherings, found in Paul's correction of the Corinthian *ekklesia*:

> What then shall we say, brothers? When you come together, everyone has a hymn, or a word of instruction, a revelation, a tongue or an interpretation. All of these must be done for the strengthening of the church. If anyone speaks in a tongue, two—or at the most three— should speak, one at a time, and someone must interpret. If there is no interpreter, the speaker should keep quiet in the church and speak to himself and God. Two or three prophets should speak, and the others should weigh carefully what is said. And if a revelation comes to someone who is sitting down, the first speaker should stop. For you can all prophesy in turn so that everyone may be instructed and encouraged. The spirits of prophets

> are subject to the control of prophets. For God is not a
> God of disorder but of peace. (1 Corinthians 14:26-33)

Notice that the first century church had no need of a deacon assigned to keep people awake! Also conspicuously absent? Assigned seating, a "high place" to stand on, a preplanned "order of worship," a ceremony around the "eucharist," a "worship leader" or "audience"—in short, all of the features of "worship services" in the third century and beyond. When Christians gathered in the first century, there was no assigned *anything*. There was no *preplanned* anything. There was no designated reader or speaker or teacher who always gave the "message of the hour." The time together was free-flowing, dynamic, and interruptible ("when revelation comes to someone who is sitting down, the first speaker should stop"). The Spirit of Jesus, rather than tradition, ran the meeting. Each believer was a participant. Each person considered what gift he or she could offer to build up the entire Body. Everyone came prepared to share.

Gatherings in the third century were safe; gatherings in the first century sometimes weren't. That's why Paul had to offer correction! There was risk. But there was also *life*. Life! When God's people gathered, they discovered Him afresh in one another. They walked and talked with Him "in the cool of the day" together, as He had always longed for His people to do.

Beginnings of "Clergy" and "Laity"

In the matter of "holy men," the developments may be even more disquieting. In a radical break with New Testament experience and teaching, a defined religious hierarchy was beginning to emerge. By the end of the third century, we find each local assembly governed by a single "bishop," wielding a high level of authority and enjoying a lifetime appointment.

It was absolutely *not* always so. As we have seen, Jesus forbade religious titles of any kind. Even the apostles were not to "lord it over" or "exercise authority" over others. Jesus took great pains to remind them, "You have only one Master and you are all brothers." Throughout the first century, leaders of great ability and faith nevertheless honored Jesus' command. When a local leader in an assembly stepped over the line and began "loving to be first," an apostle was quick to warn and rebuke him (3 John 9).

It is true that Paul had recognized elders in each *ekklesia* when he revisited it some years after its birth. These "elders" were to nurture, feed, and protect those who were "younger" in the faith. But these older believers were never to emulate the gentile model of "authority," and never did they degenerate into one-man rule or settle into a hierarchy. Paul's farewell to the elders of his beloved Ephesus is clear: a group of men—perhaps even a roomful—called "elders" in the text were exhorted, "Keep watch over yourselves and all the flock of which the Holy Spirit has made you overseers. Be shepherds of the church of God, which He bought with His own blood." In a passage of inspired scripture, we find the same men referred to as "elders," "shepherds," and "overseers"—the words that have been rendered in traditional religious vocabulary as "presbyters," "pastors," and "bishops." But in the world of Paul, these Greek words had *no* religious connotations whatsoever. They were certainly not "titles" designating "office" or "position." They were simply descriptions of people who had the capacity for mature faith and discernment (elders), who could feed and protect God's lambs (shepherds), and who were spiritually "taller" and therefore capable of greater vision and a clearer perspective (overseers). These word-pictures always described a group of men who by virtue of gifting and maturity were able to serve the local *ekklesia*. They never describe a one-man rule.

We know enough historical details to at least sketch the evolution of the creature known as a third-century bishop. In the 90's, a letter from a Christian in Rome to the church in Corinth still used the term "bishops" in plural for men in the local assembly. But by 110, a letter sent to the largest churches in the province of Asia—many of whom had received a letter from Jesus Himself in Revelation just a generation earlier—mentions a single bishop in each. Not everyone felt enthusiastic support of the emerging hierarchy. The "Shepherd of Hermas," written about this same time, closes with a figure symbolizing the Church issuing this warning: "Now therefore I say unto you that are rulers of the Church, and that occupy the chief seats; be not like the sorcerers. The sorcerers indeed carry their drugs in boxes, but you carry your drug and your poison in your heart"—the poison, it is implied, of ambition.

But in the second century, the signs steadily grew more alarming. Ignatius wrote that the bishop was "the image of the Father" and that the man who didn't recognize him as such "deceives not the bishop, who is seen, but deceives God, who is invisible." People should even feel "reverence" for a bishop. Those who tried to act independently of a bishop's authority were "servants of the devil." Or as Cyprian put it in the third century, opposition to God's "minister" was opposition to God Himself. By the mid-third century, the "laity" in Rome were reported to say, "One God, one Christ, one Holy Spirit, and in a church there ought to be one bishop."

The teacher Origen took a dim view of this development:

> We [leaders] terrify people and make ourselves inaccessible, especially if they are poor. To people who come to ask us to do something for them, we behave as no tyrant, even, would: we are more savage to petitioners than any civil rulers are. You can see this happening in many recognized churches, especially in the bigger cities. (Origen, Commentary on Matthew 16:8)

Surely others opposed the development of the professional "holy man" in Christianity; if everything had gone smoothly, men like Ignatius would never have felt the need to prop up the bishops' authority. Yet year by year, the "bishopric" came more and more to resemble an ecclesiastical dictatorship.

Even in the third century, bishops did not wear distinctive clothing, nor did they receive salaries. They might receive a share in the free-will offerings of the believers, but they were not guaranteed wages. Salaries during that period were only found in certain heretical groups and were considered scandalous among the churches. And there was no notion of a hierarchy larger than the local assembly; there was no "bishop of bishops" during these centuries. Yet the slide down the slippery slope of religion was already picking up speed. From this point on, the rarely questioned assumption of most professing Christians was that they *needed* a professional, titled clergyman to stand between mere "laity" and their God.

It was during this same period that Christians took another large step towards surrendering their birthright of an intimate, immediate relationship with Jesus. Ironically, it came through the one thing we most admire about the believers during this era— their courage and steadfastness in spite of persecution. To this day, we are still stirred by the trust and tranquility of believers like Perpetua or Polycarp, even in the face of torture and death.

It's not hard to imagine the impact of the martyrs' faith on their contemporaries. Christians who were imprisoned for their beliefs, yet continued to speak boldly for Jesus while awaiting sentencing and execution, were honored as superheroes of the faith. It was widely believed that Christians on "death row" enjoyed an unmatched closeness to God. Surely, then, their prayers would be especially effective. Fellow believers began begging their imprisoned brothers and sisters to pray for personal sins or other concerns. After their execution, martyrs were continually held up as exemplary Christians in nearly every assembly. The dates of their deaths were remembered and commemorated each year, reinforcing the "special day" mentality that was taking root among the local assemblies.

The whole concept of martyrdom steadily grew more twisted. Melito, who carried the title of "bishop of Sardis" in the late second century, wrote: "There are two things which give remission of sins: baptism and suffering for the sake of Christ." Tertullian, the North African leader, put it even more bluntly just a generation later: "Your blood is the key to Paradise." Some Christians even began *volunteering* for martyrdom, much to the puzzlement of pagan governors.

By the third century, people had begun collecting mementos of martyred believers—bits of clothing, personal effects, even bones—partly for the inspiration, partly as "spiritual good luck charms." People took the notion of asking martyrs for prayers even further. Visitors to their graves would request intercessory prayer from the dead believers. The practice of "venerating saints" and their relics had begun.

The consequences to faith were monumental. Veneration was another layer of insulation separating people from intimacy with God. On earth, the burgeoning hierarchy stood between God and man. In heaven, the growing honor roll of "saints" did the same. The "right here, right now" closeness to Jesus that the early disciples had enjoyed—both before and after His ascension—was itself becoming a relic of the past.

The "Conversion" of Constantine

He was one of the few truly pivotal figures in history. In a very real sense, he founded a religion. His name was Constantine.

His father had been designated one of four co-rulers of the Roman Empire. Constantine was bitterly hurt that he had not also been included among the four. He accompanied his father to the Roman outpost in Britain and bided his time. When his father died, Constantine had the troops proclaim him a new co-emperor. For the next three years, he fought and maneuvered his way to greater power. Finally, in the year 312, Constantine was ready to move his troops south in hopes of taking the big prize: Rome. To get to the city, his army had to cross Milvian Bridge, a stone structure across the Tiber River. His rival's army came out of the city to defend the bridge. It was there that *something* happened that would affect church history for at least the next two thousand years.

We do not have Constantine's personal account of the events. We only have the story told by two of his acquaintances.

Just four years after the event, Lactantius, the future tutor to the emperor's sons, wrote that Constantine had seen a dream "on the eve of battle" in which he had been ordered to mark his soldiers' shields with the "heavenly sign of God."

We also have the Roman senate's version of the events, preserved for us in a monument known as the Arch of Constantine. Built in 315, only three years after Constantine's "conversion" and subsequent victory, the arch shows the earliest known record of the events. Its inscription simply states that Constantine had won his battles "at the instigation of divinity," without specifying *which* divinity the senate had in mind. The emperor's personal guard is depicted, but there is no "sign of the cross" on their shields. Above them hover the traditional images of the pagan "gods." The senators were pagans creating a monument for other pagans. Perhaps that is why they omitted from the arch any reference to Christianity. Still, it seems strange that Constantine never had the monument "corrected," if indeed he found it offensive.

Eusebius, writing a full quarter century later and at least a dozen years after hearing Constantine's description of the events, told a much more elaborate version. He stated that the future emperor had learned that his political rival in Rome was using spells and sacrifices to drum up support from the pagan gods. Constantine was feeling the need for divine aid for his army, too. It was then, according to Eusebius, that Constantine and "all the troops" saw the sign of the cross in the noonday sky, with the legend "By this, conquer" emblazoned under it. That night, it was claimed, Constantine saw Jesus in a dream, ordering him to use the sign of the cross "in his engagements with the enemy." The next day, Constantine ordered his men to paint a cross on their shields. He now launched the attack, which succeeded beyond his wildest dreams. The empire was his.

We will never know for sure exactly what happened at Milvian Bridge in 312. But we can say this with certainty: none of the three narrations of the "event," whether chiseled in stone by Roman pagans or written on parchment by professing Christians, make any mention of sin, the Blood, forgiveness, repentance, reconciliation, or a new birth. It is a strange "conversion."

For many years afterwards, Constantine demonstrated a broad toleration, to the point of compromise, with the majority pagan religion. He retained the traditional imperial title of *pontifex maximus,* the high priest of the ancient Roman pagan religion.[2] The image of the pagan "sun god," worshipped by Constantine's father and previous emperors, appears three times on the Arch of Constantine. Official imperial documents, including coinage, continued to display this "sun god" until 324.

In 325, Constantine convened two "ecumenical church councils" to deal with the problem of heresy. Bishops and other leaders were summoned from all over the empire. In a speech attributed to him at the first of these councils, Constantine quoted freely and at great length from two pagan religious sources, one a legendary prophetess and the other a classical Roman poet. Remarkably, he not only took their words as authoritative but even tried to extract Christian principles and proof texts from them. The very next year, when a prominent pagan priest wished to make a pilgrimage to Egypt to see an idol that was said to make noises like a human voice, Constantine footed the bill.

Constantine disliked the city of Rome, so he decided to build a new capital, Constantinople, in the east. At its dedication in 330, he arranged for a ceremony that was half Christian, half pagan, and placed an image of the cross over the chariot of the "sun god" in the marketplace.

It was not until shortly before his death in 337 that Constantine was finally baptized. He apparently was afraid that sins committed after baptism would not be forgiven and so waited until the last possible moment to perform the ritual, as he understood it.

There were indeed sins to be concerned about. Shortly after Constantine took Rome, his former ally—now perceived as a competitor—was found strangled to death. In 326, Constantine executed his eldest son because of scandalous accusations against him. A few months later, when he realized he had been misled about the young man, he executed the accuser—his own wife, Fausta. There can be little doubt that Constantine was ambitious and ruthless when it came to securing and protecting his image and position.

Such was Constantine's "conversion" and its effect on his life. Yet while the *authenticity* of his conversion can be questioned, the impact of it cannot. The emperor threw himself into his new cause with characteristic energy, passion, and shrewdness. The changes that he brought to his religion during a single generation are nothing short of revolutionary.

The "Conversion" of Christianity

Constantine's goal was to unify his empire under the "the sign of the cross." He viewed himself as a creature of destiny, a mighty instrument in God's hands. In an open letter, dated about 324, he wrote:

> Surely it cannot be deemed arrogance in one who has received benefits from God, to acknowledge them in the loftiest terms of praise. I myself, then, was the instrument whose services He chose, and esteemed suited for the accomplishment of His will. Accordingly, beginning at the remote Britannic ocean…through the aid of divine power I banished and utterly removed every form of evil which prevailed, in the hope that the human race, enlightened through my instrumentality, might be recalled to a due observance of the holy laws of God, and at the same time our most blessed faith might prosper under the guidance of His almighty hand. (Eusebius, *Life of Constantine II*, Chapter 28)

These are the words of a man who viewed himself in almost Messianic terms. He was a man with a mission: to root out evil and enlighten the human race, so that Christianity might prosper. How would he accomplish such a lofty goal?

For starters, he would build "church buildings."

At the start of the fourth century, only a few local assemblies had made the conceptual leap from gathering in remodeled private houses to erecting religiously-purposed buildings. We know from historical documents of one town in Egypt with two "church buildings," one synagogue, and twelve pagan temples. An eyewitness to the great persecution in Egypt in 303 tells of three other cities where "basilicas" of some type were burned down. Still, these were unimpressive structures, probably of simple wooden construction. They were not fit for an imperial religion, apparently.

Constantine began his career as a builder by erecting a huge statue of himself, "ten times larger than life," holding a "lofty spear in the shape of a cross" in the busiest section of Rome. He then constructed his first of many "church buildings," also in Rome. It was magnificent, a palace, really: the Lateran Basilica, which eventually passed to the control of the "bishop of Rome" and to this day belongs to the Roman pope.

His mother, Helena, also encouraged and helped bankroll this fourth-century building program. She had made a "pilgrimage" to Palestine in 326, immediately after the executions of her daughter-in-law and grandson. Upon her return, Helena built an elaborate basilica around a room in her imperial palace, covering its floor with soil from Jerusalem. It was intended to serve as a shrine for the souvenir relics she brought back from the "holy land." Included among the trinkets, it was said, was a bone from Thomas' index finger, the very digit that he used to test Jesus' wounds. The shrine is still standing today.

So began an unprecedented wave of religious construction. For the next twenty-five years, Constantine financed a series of magnificent, lavish religious structures throughout the empire. He ordered the bishop of Jerusalem to build at public expense a "Church of the Holy Sepulchre" on the supposed site of Golgotha. He also constructed a mammoth basilica over a shrine in Rome where Peter was believed to be buried. He continued by building similar shrines, rivaling any pagan temple in magnificence, in Bethlehem, Mamre, Nicomedia, and Heliopolis. His own city, Constantinople, was not to be left out. Gradually, it became filled with martyrs' shrines, taking the place of the polytheistic shrine on every street corner that the pagans had always known.

Constantine did not confine himself to constructing "special places," however. He made his mark in legislating "special days" as well. In 321, he decreed that *dies Solis*—the day of the sun, or "Sunday"—would be a day of rest throughout the empire:

> On the venerable day of the Sun let the magistrates and people residing in cities rest, and let all workshops be closed. In the country however persons engaged in agriculture may freely and lawfully continue their pursuits because it often happens that another day is not suitable for grain-sowing or vine planting; lest by neglecting the proper moment for such operations the bounty of heaven should be lost. (Constantine, Decree of March 7, 321)

Here again we see a curious blend between paganism and Christianity, as Constantine conceived it. The "venerable day" of the sun-god, the deity Constantine's father had worshipped, was now to be commemorated with a Sabbath-like observance. The concept of a "Sunday service" had been taken to a completely new level, with the opportunity to take a day off work and meet in the luxurious new "church buildings."

Constantine was certainly making his mark. But his biggest impact perhaps came in his vision for the developing clergy. Constantine gave them enormous privilege and power. In the cities of the Roman empire, the funds for most public works, including games and celebrations, came not from taxes, but from the personal fortunes of officeholders. "Love of your hometown," if you were a member of the Roman upper class, meant spending huge amounts of your personal wealth to finance public works. It was in essence a very steeply graduated income tax. Legally, no substantial property owner was exempt. Constantine changed the custom with the stroke of a pen. From 313 on, bishops and Christian "clergy" were exempted from the burden of holding office. So great was this financial reward, that the emperor had to issue a second decree forbidding wealthy pagans from pretending to be bishops so that they could avoid public service!

At the same time, he broadly extended the bishops' powers. In a civil or even criminal suit, a bishop could issue a judgment that was binding on any other court of law. Constantine also convened empire-wide meetings of clergy to legislate on particular religious questions. Increasingly, the clergy imitated the form and function of a secular government. At the end of the third century, Roman governors had been given deputies called "vicars" and provinces had been grouped into bigger regions called "dioceses." These words were appropriated by the growing religious bureaucracy only a generation later. Under Constantine, the religious hierarchy was growing from a local expression to a global one.

What had begun, then, as a gradual slide down a slippery slope in the second and third centuries had accelerated into a freefall by the fourth. Christianity had been transformed into a religion. It certainly bore all the hallmarks of human religion, with special places, days, and men. Constantine had done much to formulate and promote this change. But perhaps his biggest impact was in opening the doors of the church to a new breed of "convert" much like himself. "Church" in the fourth century meant something radically different than it had to Paul or Peter or John. "Membership" was now politically correct. It was even fashionable, the logical choice for the upwardly mobile Roman young professional who wished to get ahead in the brave new "Christian empire." Above all, the church was now viewed as something *attendable*. Instead of meeting furtively in private homes, fearing the pounding on the door that would signify the start of another round of persecution, these new "Christians" could gather openly in some of the most magnificent buildings in the empire. And instead of sharing life together, seven days a week, it was now possible to "attend services" on the "venerable day of the Sun" without interfering too much with one's private life.

It was easier to be this sort of Christian than not. And by the time Rome fell and the "dark ages" began, *every single person* in continental Europe—with the exception of a few Jewish holdouts—would profess to be a Christian.

The Accommodation of Paganism

Because of Constantine and the leaders who came after him, the clergy had a perplexing problem on their hands. "Christianity," as Constantine had envisioned it, was to become the state religion. Citizenship in the empire (and in the kingdoms that followed it) would eventually become equated with membership in the "catholic" (i.e., universal) church. But how do you "christianize" the citizens of a pagan empire, many of whom were now "converting" in the hopes of social advancement or in the face of heavy peer pressure—or even at the point of the sword?

In the first few generations of Christianity, every single person who joined his or her heart with the *ekklesia* did so voluntarily, despite pressure from antagonistic, deeply entrenched political and religious powers. The vigor of this complete abandonment, freely given, was undeniable. Christians not only endured a hostile environment—they thrived in it. As the writer of Hebrews put it,

> Remember those earlier days after you had received the light, when you stood your ground in a great contest in the face of suffering. Sometimes you were publicly exposed to insult and persecution; at other times you stood side by side with those who were so treated. You sympathized with those in prison and joyfully accepted the confiscation of your property, because you knew that you yourselves had better and lasting possessions. (Hebrews 10:32-34)

The *ekklesia* lived as a close-knit family who had counted the cost of commitment, yet had decided to follow Jesus anyway, *because they thought He was worth it.*

Christianity as a state religion was quite different, however. The "church" was now supposed to encompass a vast populace who frankly might prefer their pagan religion but were "joining" the new one because they felt they had to. Hence the problem facing the religious leaders: How do you *force* loyalty? How do you get someone to *like* something they don't *love?* How do you make someone *reject* a pagan religion externally when they still *embrace* it internally?

One strategy is *instruction,* under the assumption that people want to hang on to pagan beliefs and practices only because they are ignorant of the beliefs of a "better" religion. The strategy was applied, with extremely limited success. The assumption proved to be a naïve one. Most people preferred their old life to the new, even when the new was explained to them.

A second strategy is *coercion.* Throughout the middle ages, in various times and places, from the local actions of religious leaders right up to the widespread horrors of the Inquisition, coercion was applied, often with a great deal of diligence. But wiser heads eventually discovered the truth: compulsion can produce a grudging, external compliance, but it can never effect heart-level change. Coercion and conversion are, in fact, complete opposites.

A third strategy is *accommodation.* If most people prefer the old way of life, one can simply try to adjust the "new" way of life to look, sound, and feel like the old. The religious leadership embraced this strategy—sometimes subconsciously, but often quite deliberately—and at last achieved the results they hoped for. Many pagan religious elements were introduced into Christianity, with their most objectionable qualities sanitized and their most sentimentally valued qualities "christianized" with new names and modestly tweaked practices. Christianity was little by little nudged closer to the old pagan religions, until the populace of Europe by and large felt that the newer religion was sufficiently within their comfort zones to be acceptable.

Jesus, of course, had different a different idea. He never desired to create a state religion—or any other religion, for that matter. He described His way, the way to Life, as a narrow and difficult road. The road was open to anyone, but only a few would ever decide to venture on it (Matthew 7:14). Jesus' strategy was primarily a *proclamation* and *demonstration* of the Kingdom of God and an *invitation* to "any who had ears to hear" to abandon their previous lives and embrace His. He had no need of coercion and no interest whatsoever in accommodation. He already knew that "tidying up" a religion through minor adjustments and repairs simply wouldn't work. As He explained:

> No one tears a piece of cloth from a new garment and uses it to patch an old garment. For then the new garment would be ruined, and the new patch wouldn't even match the old garment. And no one puts new wine into old wineskins. For the new wine would burst the wineskins, spilling the wine and ruining the skins. New wine must be stored in new wineskins. But no one who drinks the old wine seems to want the new wine. "The old is just fine," they say. (Luke 5:36-39)

The religious officials of the fourth through fourteenth centuries largely ignored this advice. They had to. They had an agenda of transforming Christianity into a religion that everyone could and would accept. Somehow, they had to transform Christianity into a superhighway that everyone would travel on, even if the travelers would have preferred something else. To achieve that goal, they tore patches from the religion of Jesus and tried to cover up the most embarrassing holes in paganism. They poured the new wine of Jesus into the old skins of traditional European religion. They achieved their goal; the populace finally complied with the new state religion.

True, the new wine was spilled. But most folks thought the old wine was just fine, anyway.

7

CHRISTENDOM AT THE NEW MILLENNIUM

Much can happen in seventeen centuries. Crusades. Inquisitions. Reformations. Movements. Missionaries. All of these developments had an impact on history; each has been the subject of countless volumes of scholarly analysis. The bottom line for us, though, is to realize that Christianity in its first few centuries offers us *two* legacies to choose from.

One heritage dates back to the earliest days, when a group of men and women lived with Jesus, experiencing Him every moment that they lived and every place that they went. These early disciples then introduced to a generation of believers the same whole-life submission to Jesus and enjoyment of Him. This corporate experience was called the *ekklesia*.

The second heritage dates back almost as far. It involves compartmentalizing life into "special" days and secular days, "special" places and common places, "special" people and laypeople, "religion" and "real life." The second version of Christianity grew up in parallel with the first, gradually overcoming it in the second and third centuries and overwhelming it in the fourth.

Where, then, do we stand today, as Christianity enters into a new millennium? What is life like for most professing Christians? Are their lives infused with an experience of Jesus and each other, during every moment and in every place? Or do special places, times, and people still dominate their thinking and actions?

Religion and Real Estate

Contemporary adherents of the Christian religion can boast facilities that rival anything that Constantine or medieval cathedral-builders ever achieved.

In Southern California sits a landmark religious facility constructed from 10,000 panes of glass. This "cathedral," designed by a world-famous architect, was built over a three-year period for a sum equivalent to $55 million in 2007. The pastor of this early "megachurch" financed it in large part by selling individual panes of glass for $500 each. The colossal structure, which can seat 3000, is also known for one of the largest pipe organs in the world.

On the other side of the planet sits a megachurch religious facility with an entirely different exterior: titanium. Completed in 2002 for $27 million, it seats 2300 people in a facility modeled after the Guggenheim museum in Bilbao, Spain. It features a café, a putting green, a rooftop garden, and a lounge area complete with built-in plasma televisions. The auditorium covers 18,000 square feet. Its stage has a bright LED screen and two adjoining makeup rooms.

In 2005, the largest megachurch in North America moved into a building that was formerly home to professional basketball team. The non-denominational assembly began meeting in 1959 in an abandoned feed store. Today, it meets in the 16,000 seat arena, renovated over a 15-month period for $75 million. During the service, three gigantic screens display video clips, while the preacher speaks in front of a giant rotating golden globe.

These modern day "basilicas" are simply the most visible examples of one of the integral features of modern Christendom: the "church building." They are certainly not the only examples, however. In the United States alone, there were at the dawn of the new millennium at least *a quarter of a million* congregations claiming to represent the Christian religion[3]. Some of these groups shared buildings; others rented public facilities, like schools or movie theaters. But most met in their own dedicated facilities, ranging from the humble urban storefront to the elaborate glass cathedral. At a conservative estimate, close to 200,000 church buildings dot the American landscape. The value of real estate belonging to U.S. religious bodies is estimated to exceed $6 billion.

Jesus once told a naïve volunteer disciple, "Foxes have dens to live in, and birds have nests, but the Son of Man has no place even to lay His head" (Luke 9:58). How is it, then, that there are now 200,000 structures that all claim to be the "house of God"? In the New Testament, we read of individuals and *ekklesias* sacrificing financially to "remember the poor" (Galatians 2:10, 2 Corinthians 8-9) and to further the proclamation of the gospel (Philippians 4:10-20). In the twenty-first century, we see believers investing billions of dollars in bricks and mortar—or occasionally glass and titanium.

No one is suggesting that the Bible *forbids* religious structures. We are definitely suggesting, however, that in the entire New Testament, not a single Christian ever built one. *It apparently never occurred to them.*

One of the fastest growing religious movements in the western world is trying to dispense with the "church building" concept altogether. According to a 2006 survey[4], about 5% of all Americans who belong to a Christian religious body of some type attend *only* house churches. A further 19% have a foot in both worlds, attending both a house church and a conventional congregation regularly. The average house church has only twenty regular attendees, with seven of them children. Three-fourths of the participants have been involved for less than a year. Most view the change as a positive experience, reporting a higher level of satisfaction than their conventional counterparts with the quality of their leadership, the faith commitment of their fellow members, and the spiritual depth they have experienced.[5]

But the operative word in the previous paragraph may well be "attend." True, they meet in a house or some other venue than a traditional church building. But most of them have essentially moved their "Sunday services" into a living room, with few substantial changes beyond the smaller size and less formal surroundings. A full 80% of house churches always meet at the same time each week, and 62% never vary their meeting format. Here is a question that is rather difficult to assess in these survey results: How many of the house church members have lives that are deeply intertwined outside the meetings? Or to ask the question conversely, how many house church members still live fragmented, compartmentalized lives? How many still think and live as if "church" were *located* in a particular place?

Santa, the Easter Bunny, and the "Venerable Day of the Sun"

In Western society, the calendar seemingly centers on a holiday known as "Christmas." How would an outside observer make sense of this celebration? On the one hand, it's about a baby lying in a feed trough, commemorated by a solid month of non-stop music (pa-rumpa-pum-pum). On the other, it's about an elderly arctic resident who violates every law of physics, crisscrossing the globe in a single night at velocities approaching the speed of light, traveling in a sled powered by flying deer. This rotund gentleman is said to break and enter each home, either by descending through the chimney or by some other security breach, and deliver gifts. Our outside observer would doubtless be relieved and puzzled to learn that this man is simply part of an elaborate mythology that is passed on as truth to trusting children by seemingly responsible adults. It would be understandable if the observer asked whether the other story—the one about the baby—was also just a fairytale.

No wonder, then, that Westerners who grew up with the competing stories seem to find the "true meaning of Christmas" a bit elusive. The "spirit" of the season is supposed to have something to do with joy, generosity, and general niceness, but the details are a little hard to pin down. As Shaw once said, "What a man believes may be ascertained, not from his creed, but from the assumptions on which he habitually acts." Maybe, then, we can understand what people *really* believe about Christmas by watching what they habitually do during the season.

Most people, it turns out, shop and party.

During the first ten months of 2006, Census Bureau statistics show that retail department stores in the USA hummed along with $10 billion in sales each month. In November, department stores began singing a new tune, the familiar melody of ringing cash registers set to a rotating soundtrack of the same thirty "Christmas songs," played incessantly over the loudspeaker. It's music to shop by. Sales figures rose to $13 billion in November, and then skyrocketed to nearly $18 billion in December—most of that in the first three weeks.

Other retail outlets enjoyed similar sales increases during the "holiday shopping season." Americans paid half a billion dollars for live Christmas trees and shelled out even more for ornaments. In December, sporting goods, electronics, and computer sales nearly doubled over an average month, while jewelry sales nearly tripled. The postal service delivered twelve million packages *each day* during the season. Liquor stores, not be left out, reported a huge increase in sales, from under $3 billion monthly most of the year to a whopping $4.5 billion in December.

Could it be that self-indulgence, characterized by materialism and alcohol consumption, is "the true meaning of Christmas"? The standard Christian answer—at least during the past several decades—would be an indignant, "Jesus is the reason for the season." Secularists, it is maintained, pulled off a hostile takeover of the holiday, but at its heart Christmas is still about Christ.

But does history bear out that assumption?

To answer that question, we must again examine Roman paganism. They worshipped a "deity" named Saturn, who is best remembered for devouring his children at birth, for fear that one might grow up to overthrow him. Romans celebrated this monster with Saturnalia, a weeklong festival marked by revelry and materialism that was observed December 17-24 each year. In AD 50, the stoic thinker Seneca the Younger wrote, "It is now the month of December, when the greatest part of the city is in a bustle. Loose reins are given to public dissipation; everywhere you may hear the sound of great preparations." The fourth century writer Libanius observed about Saturnalia, "The desire to spend money grips everybody...A stream of presents pours itself out on all sides." Sound familiar?

The Romans were also sun worshipers. In the early third century, they began celebrating a festival called *Dies Natalis Solis Invicti,* "the birthday of the unconquered sun," observed on December 25. On that date they could detect the days starting to lengthen ever so slightly, evidence that the sun was "unconquered" by the night. When emperor Aurelian took the sun to be his "patron god" in the late third century, he promoted December 25 as an empire-wide holiday.

In contrast, there is no historical evidence whatsoever that Christians celebrated the birth of Jesus with any holiday before the fourth century. The date of His birth is not recorded in the scriptures. The only hint we have is in Luke's gospel, where we learn that shepherds were "living out in the fields nearby, keeping watch over their flocks at night"—strong evidence that Jesus' birth took place during the warmer months between late spring and early fall. A December date just doesn't fit. How is it, then, that the "nativity" came to be observed at Saturnalia, on the very date pagans set aside as the "nativity" of the so-called sun god? We will let a well known twelfth-century Syrian religious leader, Jacob Bar-Salibi, explain:

> It was a custom of the pagans to celebrate on the same 25 December the birthday of the sun, at which they kindled lights in token of festivity. In these solemnities and revelries the Christians also took part. Accordingly when the doctors of the Church perceived that the [nominal] Christians had a leaning to this festival, they took counsel and resolved that the true Nativity should be solemnized on that day. (cited in Ramsay MacMullen, 1997, Christianity and Paganism in the Fourth to Eighth Centuries, p. 155, Yale)

Christmas, then, is an example of the substitution strategy by which pagan customs were "christianized" and welcomed into Christianity. The "birthday of the sun god" morphed into "the birthday of the Son of God," and the revelry and materialism of Saturnalia morphed into the revelry and materialism of Christmas. The names changed, but the *heart* remained the same.

And what of the other traditions we associate with the December 25 holiday? They, too, came from European pagan customs, attracted to Christmas because they came from celebrations held about the same time. "Yule" was an ancient winter festival of the pagan Scandinavians, who burned "yule logs" to honor their "thunder god." Kissing under the mistletoe is the remnant of an ancient fertility rite in Britain, held each winter when the plant bore its fruit. "Christmas trees" are probably the vestige of an ancient German pagan practice of tree decoration during their winter fertility celebration.

The elderly arctic resident, "Santa Claus," is a product of a Darwinian evolution of sorts. Several pagan religions of northern Europe worshipped beings with similar descriptions. These traditions merged with the story of Nicholas, a fourth-century Christian who was known for giving gifts to the poor. The final ingredient in our Santa is "Father Christmas," an English figure who originally symbolized holiday drunkenness and revelry but who received an image makeover during the Victorian period. Throw in the artwork of a nineteenth-century American cartoonist, Thomas Nast, and the evolution of a modern myth is complete.

This brief history of Christmas raises the question: How is it possible to "keep the Christ in Christmas," when He was never there at the start? And how is it possible to "take the Saturn out of Saturnalia"—along with all the other pagan elements—when that's where those traditions originated?

Other holidays taken for granted by most Westerners, professing Christian and secular humanist alike, have similar stories.

In North America on October 31 each year, hordes of costumed children troop through their neighborhoods collecting candy. The most popular disguises are skeletons, corpses, movie murderers, occult figures, and stylized representations of the devil. "Ghost stories" make the rounds. Each year, Hollywood promotes the latest installment of sadistic horror movie franchises offering mutilation and murder as entertainment. Vandalism is also commonplace. In some metropolitan areas, the preceding evening, known as "devil's night" or "hell night," is celebrated with random acts of arson. Mexicans observe their "Day of the Dead" by decorating graves of deceased relatives with "offerings"—toys, alcohol, food, or trinkets—intended as gifts for the dead. Vendors in the streets sell skeleton-shaped trinkets. Candy confections known as "sugar skulls" are given as gifts. Rabbit, decorated with white frosting to look like a deformed skeleton, is a favorite meal.

Most citizens in these cultures look on the celebrations with fond sentimentality. Most also profess to be Christians. How can this be? Isn't there an enormous contradiction between the values of Jesus and these blatantly pagan "holy days"?

The pagan Celts inhabited Britain two millennia ago. Their occult religion included an autumn festival commemorating death. The shorter days and colder weather signified the end of life for the crops in the field and the leaves on the trees. The Celts believed that the barriers separating the living and the dead broke down for one night. They were convinced that the deceased spirits would seek out their living relatives, and so sought to pacify these "ghosts" with approved rituals. Their contemporaries, the Romans, said that these Druidic rites included human sacrifice.

Since the Celts stubbornly refused to abandon their pagan traditions, religious officials in the eighth century decided to offer them a substitute, "All Saints' Day," on November 1. It was still a day to honor the dead, but the leaders tried to focus the attention on departed Christian heroes. In the eleventh century, a second accommodation to paganism was proposed. An "All Souls' Day" was added, so that people could honor any dead relative, not just "saints." This two-day religious festival became known as "Hallowmas" and the evening before as "All Hallows' Eve." Popular use shortened the name to "Halloween."

The whitewash applied to paganism soon wore off, it seems. Today, hardly anyone in North America takes the "Christian" aspects of All Saints Day or All Souls Day seriously. But the pagan aspects of the day are still thriving every October 31.

With the creation of "Hallowmas" and "Halloween," the officials had found a successful strategy to stop Celtic religious tradition. But they had ended it not by changing hearts, or even habits. Instead, they had simply *changed its name,* added some Christian trappings, and welcomed it into the Christian religion! But does this strategy amount to Christianizing paganism, or is it really just paganizing Christianity instead?

What about Easter? Surely no "special day" is more Christian than the annual celebration of the resurrection, right? It is true that by the middle of the second century—two generations after the apostles—some sort of yearly observance of the resurrection was becoming common among believers. But this practice does *not* trace its history back to the earliest church. A well-known fifth century historian, who himself observed the holiday, offered an insightful commentary about its origins:

> Inasmuch as men love festivals, because they afford them cessation from labor: each individual in every place, according to his own pleasure, has by a prevalent custom celebrated the memory of the saving passion. The Savior and his apostles have enjoined us by no law to keep this feast: nor do the Gospels and apostles threaten us with any penalty, punishment, or curse for the neglect of it, as the Mosaic law does the Jews. It is merely for the sake of historical accuracy…that it is recorded in the Gospels that our Savior suffered in the days of unleavened bread. The aim of the apostles was not to appoint festival days, but to teach a righteous life and piety. And it seems to me that just as many other customs have been established in

individual localities according to usage, so also the feast
of Easter came to be observed in each place according to
the individual peculiarities of the peoples inasmuch as
none of the apostles legislated on the matter.[6]

Did you catch that? An early catholic historian recognized that
Easter was neither taught nor practiced by the apostles, who had
no desire to establish "festival days" anyway. Instead, the men who
established Easter "according to their own pleasure" actually "love
festivals" because they get the day off from work! Easter, rather
than dating from the earliest church, was just a *custom* established
by local usage.

The New Testament indeed gives no hint—zero—that resurrection
day, as significant as it was, should be honored by an annual
celebration. There was a way that Jesus authorized His followers
to remember His body and blood: the meal of bread and wine
sometimes called the Lord's Supper. But the earliest Christians did
not tie this remembrance to a calendar date. After all, Jesus had
said to eat and drink the Supper in remembrance of Him "as often
as you take it" (1 Corinthians 11:25). For the early Christians, that
meal could (and did) occur any day of the week and on any day of
the year (Acts 2:42, 46).

For a *way of life*, the free-flowing, continual celebration of Jesus'
death and resurrection, as embodied in the Last Supper, is perfect.
But for a *religion*, some fixed date on a calendar is preferable. So as
the generations passed and Christianity began to reinvent itself as
a religion, a "special day" worked its way into the calendar. And
just as soon as a date was set, the "holiday" began merging with
pre-existing pagan rituals that were observed around the same
time of year.

The very name "Easter" (in English and German) is apparently
derived from a Germanic "goddess" called "Eostre." Ancient
pagan symbols of forgotten springtime fertility rites also attached
themselves to the festival. Young children everywhere believe
passionately in the myth of a rabbit who brings eggs. Indeed, the

"Easter Bunny" is far more widely recognized as a symbol of the holiday than are the cross or the empty tomb.

Wherever the holiday has gone, a dark celebration known as Carnival or Mardi Gras has been its fellow traveler. Mardi Gras, or "Fat Tuesday," is a carnal explosion of drunkenness, debauchery, and revelry—deliberately scheduled the day before the traditional period of fasting and self-denial preceding Easter. By the very act of setting aside a special day for sober reflection on the cross and resurrection, Christians were unintentionally setting aside another special day for depravity and decadence. Easter created Mardi Gras.

Special days have a way of doing that.

Of course no survey of Christendom's "special days" would be complete without a mention of Sunday. We have seen that Christians in the second and third centuries drifted into the tradition of the weekly worship service, something completely missing from the record of the New Testament. We have also seen that Constantine in the fourth century legislated that "the venerable day of the Sun"—*Solis Invicti* once again—be observed as a Roman day of rest. In the twenty-first century, Christian assemblies have loosened up their schedule a bit. Three-fourths of all Protestant congregations offer multiple "worship services" to choose from, to accommodate different preferences in music genre or "worship style." Some services have moved to non-traditional times, like Saturday evening. Even so, Constantine's "Sun-day" still rules the days of the religious week. As a result, Christianity in our century is still thought of as something you do in scheduled meetings that hopefully carry you through the days of your "normal" life. The paradigm hasn't really changed.

No one wants to be known as an "anti-Sunday holiday debunker." That's not really the point. What is crucial is to recognize that Christianity, as we define it in our generation, is inseparable from its special days. Those days were *not* part of the original experience of the early church. Instead, those special days were interlopers, intruders from a pagan environment that were welcomed into

Christianity in a failed attempt to "christianize" them. Religion, at its core, is all about special days. Christianity, in contrast, is about Jesus, today and every day. There is a difference.

"Special Men," Twenty-First Century Style

Christendom in the new millennium is characterized not only by "special places" (the building or the living room) and "special times" (holidays and scheduled worship days) but also by "special men." The twenty-first century version of the "special man" in protestant circles is known as the "pastor."

As we have seen, the New Testament writers used the terms "elder," "overseer," and "shepherd" interchangeably to describe the same person (Acts 20:17-28). In the KJV and other early English Bibles, however, the translators chose the archaic term "pastor" in place of the literal translation, "shepherd." Today, the English language has evolved to the point where the meanings of "shepherd" and "pastor" don't even overlap. If you met a man who told you he was a *shepherd*, you would never ask, "Which church?" And if you met a man who said he was a *pastor*, you would never respond, "How unusual! Where is your ranch?" When the Holy Spirit, speaking through the apostles, used the word "shepherd," it only meant a herdsman who tends, protects, and feeds sheep on the open range. It wasn't a religious title. It was a word-picture, designed to paint a mental image of a function—something certain believers with appropriate gifting, equipping, and maturity could provide within the local *ekklesia*.

In the first century, "shepherds" weren't hired or fired. They were simply "regular members" of a local assembly, just like everyone else. They were *recognized* as possessing the "gift of shepherd" because of the impact they were *already* having in feeding and protecting God's people. Their qualifications, as listed in the scriptures, all had to do with character, faith, and fruitfulness (1 Timothy 3; Titus 1). When the local *ekklesia* assembled, the shepherds were not the pre-arranged speakers or masters of ceremony (1 Corinthians 14:26-31). Some might have taught, but they were *not* the only teachers (Colossians 3:16; Hebrews 5:12). A shepherd might have received some sort of material support (Galatians 6:6; 1 Timothy 5:17-18), but it was a *sharing*, not a salary. Greed was never to be their motive (1 Peter 5:2). Above all, they were to function as brothers, not lording it over others but living among them as servants (Matthew 20:25-28, 23:8-12, 1 Peter 5:2).

Language has been a colossal problem for the human race ever since Babel. A little six-letter word like "pastor" connects to a thousand different experiences stored in the hearer's memory. If you showed Ephesians 4:11, for example, to a believer in the first century, he or she would see the Greek word *poimenas,* immediately think "shepherd," and a split second later associate the word with several intimately close relationships right in the local *ekklesia.* If you were to show 1 Timothy 3 to a believer in the twenty-first century, however, he or she would think "pastor" and associate it with the man who preaches, counsels, marries, and buries in the building down the street. Same scripture, yes, but two vitally different concepts. In the first century, "shepherd" was a relationship; in the twenty-first, "pastor" is the "special person" of the Christian "religion."

What is a modern pastor's job description? What does he actually do? We can get a very accurate snapshot from scientific surveys[7] that have asked those very questions. The average pastor reports that he works 46 hours per week. Here's how the pastoral work week breaks down:

- Preparing for the weekly service, including the sermon: 15 hours

- Counseling the troubled or visiting the sick: 9 hours

- Attending "business meetings" and doing administrative work: 7 hours

- Teaching classes or training people for "ministry": 6 hours

- Getting involved in community affairs or minister's associations: 3 hours

- Miscellaneous duties: 6 hours

If we removed from this average pastor's week everything that had no relevance in the *ekklesia* of the New Testament, what would be left? The earliest church had no "services" as we know them and certainly no assigned weekly sermons; scratch the first line item from the list. They had no business meetings. People were certainly "equipped for works of service," but not in training classes. Sunday schools, after all, weren't invented for another *eighteen hundred years*. And while believers who were sick or imprisoned definitely were cared for, it was considered the work of every member. The "congregation" didn't "hire" a specialist to do the bulk of it for them.

And that's the main point. It's not that the job of the professional clergy has evolved over the years as times have changed. It's that the whole concept of "professional clergy," as it is practiced in our century, is foreign to the New Testament!

Please do not read that statement as "pastor bashing." Nothing could be further from the truth. Our average pastor doubtless entered "the ministry" with the best of intentions. Perhaps he was an energetic, sincere young person who was given the opportunity to speak at "devotionals" or teach Bible studies. He wasn't polished, but he was sharing with a heartfelt desire to serve God and encourage others. People heard his sincerity and felt the warmth of his faith, and so they *were* encouraged. Before long, someone— maybe the pastor—suggested that he might want to "go into the ministry." This idea sounded wonderful to the younger man. He wanted to make a difference, and he loved God; what better career could there be than that of a "full time worker"? So he went off to Bible college or seminary, and perhaps to graduate study after that. Maybe he married someone he met in school who seemed to share his ideals and dreams. For the long years of education and training they worked and sacrificed; 60% of evangelical pastors in the United States hold a Masters degree or higher. Then at long last they were "called" to their first "pastorate" and went to work, with big dreams of "doing great things for the Lord."

For our average evangelical pastor, that moment was 20 years, nine months, and twenty-six days ago. That means he's put in around a thousand "average pastoral work weeks" of sermons, business meetings, counseling sessions, hospital visits, weddings, funerals, and "work days." We desperately need to ask: has it been good for him? Has it been good for the families in the pews? Is modern Christendom's clergy-laity system even *healthy*, never mind biblical?

Let's consider for a moment one implication of having a professional clergy. Professionals, by definition, get a salary. Our average pastor has been taking home a paycheck for over twenty years, but odds are he still feels considerable pressure in his personal finances. In evangelical denominations from coast to coast, *a pastor's pay is directly proportional to the size of his congregation.* We do have exact data[8]. For evangelical congregations in 2002, the median household income was $41,000, virtually identical with the U.S. median[9]. What about pastors? It turns out that most (63%) were employed by congregations with fewer than 100 members. On average, these clergy were paid only $22,300—a figure that made the pastor's family one of the lowest income households in the entire congregation. Congregations with 101-350 members, accounting for 32% of the sample, paid their pastors a median salary of $41,051, placing them squarely in the middle of the middle class. The one pastor out of every twenty who was fortunate enough to work for a congregation of 351-1000 members fared much more comfortably, bringing home $59,315. And the one pastor out of every 200 who worked at a large congregation with more than 1000 members earned top dollar, with a salary of $85,518—which, adjusted for inflation, would have been the equivalent of a six-figure income in 2008.

Is this picture healthy for anyone involved? Or does it invite charlatans while exposing well-intentioned but fallible human beings to temptations that no one should really have to face?

Here's one such temptation: If the pastor of a 1000-member congregation can earn six figures, what might the pastor of a 10,000-member congregation earn? As the twentieth century drew to a close, a new breed of clergyman—part entrepreneur, part preacher—began applying principles learned from the "church growth movement" with lots of energy and loads of marketing savvy. These "pastor-preneurs" dedicated themselves to creating the "user friendly" church experience. Religious facilities shed the stained glass, pews, and steeples and took on the appearance of posh shopping malls with impeccably groomed landscaping and comfy stadium style seating. Messages became more upbeat, with a decidedly self-help theme. Polished performances by professional musicians playing soft-rock melodies became the norm. Some services featured warm-up acts of comedians or other entertainers to get the audience loosened up. And the evolving "mega-churches" added new perks to membership. Interest groups for every hobby imaginable were formed. Assemblies added schools, banks, daycare facilities, pharmacies, coffee shops, mortgage lenders, counseling centers and the like in the effort to attract still more members. Multimedia extravaganzas with professional lighting and sound and choirs hundreds of members strong became commonplace.

Many (certainly not all) of these "pastor-preneurs" are now compensated much like the CEO of a 10,000-employee company. Add in income from book deals and speaking engagements, and a select few mega-church pastors have grown mega-wealthy. A 2003 *St. Louis Post-Dispatch* article described the lifestyles of several wealthy clergymen. One drove a black Rolls Royce and traveled in a $5 million dollar jet; another lived in a $3.5 million home; still another owned two mansions; yet another owned a 50-foot yacht; and a husband-wife "ministry team" owned a jet, a Cadillac Escalade, and a Mercedes-Benz sedan. A 2006 *New York Times* article reported a $13 million book deal for yet another "pastor-preneur."

Our average pastor, though—the fellow who's been toiling away at his 46-hour work week for the past 20.8 years—doesn't have to deal with the moral dilemma of whether to buy that yacht. You see, the average weekly attendance at his congregation is only 61. Half of those members say they tithe, but that still doesn't leave much once the mortgage and utility bills are paid. This average pastor and his average congregation are on the endangered species list. "Church membership" in America is not on the rise. It is, in fact, what economists call a "zero-sum game." For every winner who builds a mega-church with thousands of members, there are dozens of "average pastors" who lose members and find themselves pushed ever closer to the brink. What temptations do they face?

One, of course, is anxiety. How many pastors would leave "the ministry" if their Bible degree and resume gave them any realistic hopes of landing a secure, decent paying "secular" job?

A less obvious temptation, perhaps, is caution and compromise. Only a relatively few pastors (29.5%) say they enjoy challenging the "lay leaders" with new ideas and programs. Most (70.5%) admit that they "generally prefer to keep things running smoothly by introducing changes gradually." And when it comes time to make decisions about what the congregation's focus should be, not many (26.9%) even claim that they discuss the "theological rationale" of how *God* feels on the subject. The large majority (73.1%) acknowledge that they "primarily take into consideration how well it meets the needs of the members or *prospective* members."[10] With personal and congregational solvency teetering on the brink, the main consideration becomes keeping the current members happy and trying to recruit a few new ones. Is a system like that likely to yield men with bold, prophetic voices who will risk everything to take the church in a radically new (or radically ancient) direction?

The separation of believers into "clergy" and "laity" has another unintended but disastrous effect: the loss of genuine relationship. A first-century style shepherd functioning as a "brother among brothers" had no option but to lead out of personal relationship, by being deeply involved in others' lives and demonstrating the lessons he was trying to teach. A twenty-first-century style pastor must try to function from a position above the "laity." He has a title, an office, and a designated role as the expert in religious matters. He tries to fulfill his duties primarily through meetings—the worship service, the business meeting, the class, the counseling session—rather than through interactions in normal daily life.

That is why most pastors are quite lonely. One recent survey[11] revealed a world of insight in three simple statements. Virtually every pastor—a full 98% of those surveyed—considered himself a gifted teacher. No fewer than 80% counted themselves as "effective disciple makers." Yet a sizeable majority of pastors—more than six out of every ten—admit that they "have few if any close friends." Clearly most pastors believe that teaching and making disciples are essentially matters of information transfer. Their very role, however, isolates them from others and prevents effective *life* transfer.

This disconnect between "pastor" and "member" has serious spiritual consequences.

In a scientific survey conducted in 2006, a representative national sample of Protestant pastors was asked to evaluate the spiritual health of their congregations. The pastors on average claimed that 70% of their members made faith the top priority in their lives. One pastor out of every six went so far as to say that *90%* of their members made their relationship with God their highest priority. But when the members, the "people in the pews," were asked that same question, not *one fourth* would even make that claim about themselves! The overwhelming majority of the members of Protestant assemblies were honest enough to rank their faith below career, family, or the pursuit of happiness on their list of priorities.

Think of it—after hundreds, if not thousands, of sermons, seminars, "revivals," workshops, and Sunday school lessons, relatively few of those who have repeatedly heard the importance of making God their highest priority even *claim* to be living what they've been taught. But the teachers keep right on going, service after service, class after class, unaware that the flood of words is making little lasting impact.

God has spoken:

> This is the covenant I will make with the house of Israel after that time, declares the Lord. I will put My laws in their minds and write them on their hearts. I will be their

> God, and they will be My people. No longer will a man teach his neighbor, or a man his brother, saying, "Know the Lord," because they will all know Me, from the least of them to the greatest. (Hebrews 8:11-12)

If men *are* teaching their neighbors and brothers over and over to know the Lord, yet those who are being taught still do not know Him, or even embrace the goal of knowing Him as their highest priority, *that would be very important information to know.* This situation is no less than a violation of the New Covenant! Yet those who would seemingly most need to know the truth about the spiritual condition of their "flock" are perhaps the least aware of it.

Why this disconnect? When pastors in the survey were asked to list the specific standards they used in evaluating their members' spiritual health, the majority said they looked at the percentage of members who volunteered for some church "program" or "ministry." Nearly half also listed some sort of "conversion experience" and regular attendance to services as important criteria. No other measure was used by even a significant fraction of the pastors.

The organization that conducted the survey offered the following insights:

> The unifying thread running through pastors' responses to an open-ended survey question regarding how congregational health is assessed was that the most common measures do not assess much beyond the superficial participation of people in church or faith-related activity... Perhaps the most telling information relates to the measures that are not widely used by pastors to assess people's spiritual health. Less than one out of every ten pastors mentioned indicators such as the maturity of a person's faith in God, the intensity of the commitment to loving and serving God and people, the nature of each congregant's personal ministry, the breadth of congregational involvement in community

service, the extent to which believers have some forms of accountability for their spiritual development and lifestyle, the manner in which believers use their resources to advance the kingdom of God, how often people worship God during the week or feel as if they have experienced the presence of God, or how faith is integrated into the family experience of those who are connected with the church…There has never been a time when American society was in more dire need of the Christian Church to provide a pathway to a better future. Given the voluminous stream of moral challenges, and the rampant spiritual hunger that defines our culture today, this should be the heyday for biblical ministry. As things stand now, we have become content with placating sinners and filling auditoriums as the marks of spiritual health.[12]

And so we see the sad irony of the clergy-laity system in the new millennium. The people who most want to make a difference in the church are insulated from the people they are trying to help. They are asked to accomplish the goal with information transfer in a meeting-oriented system, and they are penalized if they dare to take risks. And truth is always risky.

A Million Tragedies

Two millennia have passed since the disciples enjoyed three years of "right here, right now" intimacy with Jesus and since an entire generation of believers "from the least to the greatest" discovered that same intimacy in the *ekklesia*. From this beginning, a radically different religion evolved. Like other world religions, this "Christianity" is built around religious observances conducted in "holy places" at "holy times" under the direction of "holy men." Cultural variation certainly exists, but it rarely strays far from this traditional paradigm.

It is absolutely critical that we ask ourselves this question: How is this twenty-first century Christianity working? What is its fruit in the lives of its members? Should we simply accept the fact that Christianity just "is what it is" and all agree to work within the system as "churchmen" rather than reformers? Or has the loss been so great and the fruit so meager that we should be alarmed? Does the politically themed bumper sticker, "If you're not outraged, you're not paying attention," apply to Christianity as well? Or is such talk merely "negativity"?

Perhaps one place to start is the newspaper. We could pick any year, really, but let's choose to look at a twelve-month period during 2005-2006. We find that three stories about well-respected "church members" stunned America, making front-page headlines from coast to coast.

First, a serial killer who had terrorized a city and taunted police for three decades was finally arrested. The depraved murderer pleaded guilty in court and then calmly described each killing in grisly detail. The shocking perversions of this torturer-killer are too vile to be described here. But the perversion was fed by an unchecked addiction to violent pornography. In this murderer's twisted life, fantasy periodically escaped into the real world.

The identity of the killer? The headline-grabbing fact was this: at the time of his arrest, he was serving as the *president* of his denominational congregation. He was caught because he had sent a computer diskette to a local newspaper, bragging about his crimes and mocking law enforcement officials for their inability to stop him. The diskette was traced to a computer from the church office.

The members of his assembly were absolutely stunned after his arrest. "I was dumbfounded, I was bewildered, I was shocked," his pastor said. "It's not possible. Not the man that I know." One member recalled how the killer had brought spaghetti sauce and salad to a "church supper" only a few days earlier. Another member called him "a very kind man," recounting his concern after her kidney operation. A five-year old boy, when he saw the man's picture on television, turned to his father, who had served as an usher with the murderer, and asked, "He tricked us, didn't he?" The father told a reporter, "I am not sure what to tell him. I am not sure what to tell myself." An official in the denominational hierarchy preached a sermon the next Sunday and said, "We feel dismay, anger, devastation, utter shock and disbelief. The very foundation of our faith is shaken."

After his arrest, the killer wrote what his pastor called "a very generic, laid back" letter to the congregation, thanking them for their support and asking them for their prayers. They posted the letter on a bulletin board in the foyer and included it in their morning announcements.

The serial murderer is now serving ten consecutive life sentences in a federal penitentiary.

Just three months after the trial ended, another tragic story grabbed the nation's headlines. An eighteen-year old boy accused of killing the parents of his fourteen-year old girlfriend and fleeing with her halfway across the country was arrested. Both children came from "Christian home schooling" families. In fact, the two fleeing teens had met the previous spring at a "home schooling" function. The fourteen-year old girl had a web site that talked about attending prayer groups and her interest in soccer and babysitting. At the time of her parents' murder, she was wearing a tee-shirt advertising a "Christian rock band." The eighteen-year-old boy also had a web site on which he quoted lyrics from a "Christian band" and discussed his enjoyment of computers, volleyball, and deer hunting.

Of course the news stories were filled with quotes from disbelieving friends. Of the girl, a peer said, "The way I knew her, she was very smart, and she was like an amazing friend. She's very Christian and I would have never thought any of this would happen." She also called the deceased parents "the nicest people I've ever met." The family's pastor described them as good people dealing with "typical" teenage issues. A neighbor added, "She seemed to be a typical all-American girl, just a sweet kid on the street."

Court documents painted a dramatically different picture, however. The teens had been "dating" for half a year and were "involved in an ongoing, secret, intimate relationship." Furthermore, they "often communicated via instant messages and text messages on the Internet." Their communication included "flirtatious messages" as well as "inappropriate images of one another via various electronic media" such as computers and cell phones.

After his arrest, the young man confessed the murders to authorities. The following year he agreed to a plea deal to avoid a trial with death penalty specifications. He was sentenced to two terms of life imprisonment.

A few more months passed, and yet another tragedy became front page news. A popular young preacher failed to show up at his congregation's mid-week services. A few concerned members went to his home and discovered his body. He had a gunshot wound in his back. The next day, police in a neighboring state found the preacher's wife and three children, just as they were pulling into a restaurant in their family van. The wife, police said, confessed to killing her husband. She had shot him and then had fled with the children while he lay dying in their home. After her arrest, the wife asked a friend from their congregation to convey to the members her apologies for what she had done.

The congregation was predictably shocked. They covered a bulletin board in the hallway with snapshots of the smiling family. "Words cannot describe how we all feel about this," said one member, calling the accused murderer the "'perfect mother, perfect wife." The member added, "The kids are just precious, and she was precious. He was the one of the best ministers we've ever had—just super charisma."

Another member agreed. The slain minister "had a really true concern about saving people's souls and inspiring people to rethink their habits," she told a newspaper. "He was such a great preacher, very uplifting and encouraging. You felt good when you walked away from his sermons…They were such a good couple—happy," she said.

The trial painted a disturbing picture of their home life. The wife was ensnared in a Nigerian check-cashing scam that she was trying to hide from her husband. The husband was portrayed as critical, overbearing, and demeaning. The wife was convicted of voluntary manslaughter, a common verdict in cases of spousal abuse, and sentenced to only two months in prison, in addition to the time she had already served since her arrest.

The congregation's members did recall the last sermon their minister ever preached, just three days before his death. The topic was "the Christian family."

All would agree that these stories are heartbreaking. But are they even germane to our discussion? Are they evidence that something is fundamentally flawed with the dominant paradigm in the Christian church of our day? Or are they mere aberrations in a basically healthy environment? Was it even fair to mention them here? After all, Christians have long maintained that they don't get a fair shake in the national news media.

But what if these stories *are* pertinent? What if they are the small but highly visible tip of a huge hidden iceberg of sin, unbelief, and moral failure—what Jesus would call "leaven"? We don't bring up these tragedies to be negative, or even to judge those who were involved. *We bring them up because we believe with all of our hearts that similar disasters can be prevented.* The solutions are available. But we won't look for them unless we are first willing to take an honest, unflinching look at our current situation.

Consider the "lay leader" whose addiction to violent perversion led him to commit unmentionable crimes. Surely he was an aberration, one in a hundred million. Wasn't he? The answer, sadly, is no. While the *crimes* he committed are so uncommon as to shock us, the *sinful addictions* that led to the crimes are very, very common.

One recent national survey[13] asked a representative sample of Americans whether they had voluntarily viewed explicit pornographic images during the previous seven days. Among the "unchurched," one out of every five admitted they had. And among the churched? The same fraction—*one of five.*

Statistics can leave us cold; they can seem like numbers on a page. So please, allow the implications of that figure to sink in. Next time you are in a religious service, look around you. If your assembly is typical, than one out of every five faces you see has looked at pornography at least once since the last week's service. Among the women, the number is probably less. Among the men, it may well be considerably more. Multiply what you see by two hundred thousand other assemblies meeting around the country. And ask yourself: What is the cost, in terms of loss of spiritual power and testimony in our world? What is the cost, in terms of pain caused to the Father's heart?

Tragically, the nation's clergy are not exempt from this spiritual plague. One evangelist with an international reputation has estimated that the percentage of pastors who attend his seminars who are addicted to pornography is also *one in five.*[14]

And what of the immoral teens, whose sin cost a mom and a dad their lives? Again, the *crime* itself is thankfully quite rare. But we need to look beyond the crime and discover its root causes. The girl's parents didn't die simply of gunshot wounds to the head. They died of a lethal cocktail of poisons, including *at least:* permission for adolescent children to run off in groups or pairs alone, with no supervision and no real accountability; unmonitored use and abuse of the internet and electronic communication; allowance for romantic relationships among children a *decade* away from realistically being ready for marriage; fostering an environment in which children disciple other children; disjointedness and independence on everyone's part, with no safety net of daily relationships pressing in, asking questions, offering warning or encouragement or admonition, bringing God's Word to bear in practical ways to lives; and confusion of external "life style choices" of music and education with internal choices of genuine obedience and discipleship.

The tough question we must be willing to ask ourselves is this: how many teens, raised in the church, have lives that can be characterized by the same list?

We need to admit that the majority of teens in most churches are in deep spiritual trouble. Here the statistics can be deceptive. Teens are much more likely to participate in "church based" activities than their parents. Nationwide, six of ten teens attend services each week and one of three are involved in a youth group. But if you ask those teens if they plan to participate in a local church once they are on their own, then only *one in three* has any intentions of staying involved. *Most church-going teens say that they are only waiting until they leave home to also leave the church.*[15] And if we check on attendance rates among college students and young adults, the statistics show that most of these teens will follow up on their plans. In its 2002 annual meeting, the Southern Baptist Council on Family Life reported that 88 percent of the children raised in evangelical homes leave the church at or about age 18. For two generations, at least, we have heard the cliché about children raised in the church who attend a secular university and fall away. The children are telling us we got it wrong. Doubtless there are many challenges to faith on college campuses, as well as in the workplace. But most of the time, age eighteen is only when the children stop *attending*. Tragically, they succumbed to faith-destroying, future-robbing temptations to worldliness and unbelief years before.

Finally, what of the pastor's wife who is accused of ending her husband's brief life with a gun? Surely domestic murder is a tragic anomaly, not a norm in religious congregations.

We would agree that very few marriages end with homicide, whether among clergy or laity or pagans. But millions of marriages *do* end in a court of law. Nationwide, one-fifth of all first marriages end in divorce during the first five years and one-third end during the first ten years. No less than 43% end in divorce or separation during the first fifteen years. Anyone who has experienced a divorce in their immediate family or witnessed one in the life of a close friend can testify to the pain. The hurt is both excruciating at the moment and chronic for years afterwards. Even when divorce seems unavoidable, it means heartbreak for all concerned.

Yet here is another tragedy: the divorce rate for those who consider themselves born-again Christians is *identical* with those who realize they've never been born again.[16] Please take a moment to grasp the significance of that fact. Go to any large gathering of people—say, a football game. Place on one side of the stadium all those who "have made a personal commitment to Jesus Christ that is still important in their lives today," who say that they are going to heaven when they die because they have confessed their sins and received Christ as Savior. On the other side of the stadium place all "nominal Christians," those who are unsure of their beliefs, those who are part of heretical fringe groups, all Buddhists and Muslims, all agnostics and atheists. Then ask all those who have been divorced to raise their hands.

The percentage of raised hands will be exactly the same on both sides of the stadium.

Again, we are not trying to be critical or judgmental of any individuals here. We are only saying that marriages are in just as much trouble inside the church as they are outside. Those statistics are true in spite of all the sermons, marriage seminars, pro-family parachurch organizations, books, tapes, and classes. In most assemblies in every denomination or non-denominational expression of Christianity from "sea to shining sea," a large percentage of marriages and homes are in deep, deep trouble.

It Doesn't Have To Be That Way!

We will say it again: we are not trying to criticize or judge. We are convinced that many, if not most, professing Christians involved in soul-numbing, future-robbing sins would *want* to be free from them. We wish we could grasp these people firmly by the shoulders, look them in the eye, and tell them that *it doesn't have to be that way.* They can change. The church can change.

We live in a day in which our enemy, the devil, has made disastrous inroads into our communities, our assemblies, our homes, and our private lives. *We repeat: it doesn't have to be that way!* Marriages don't have to end in heartache; children don't have to be pummeled by sin and lost to the world by the millions; the name of Jesus doesn't have to be dragged in the mud by scandal and shame. The gates of hell will not prevail against the church that Jesus will build, if we'll let Him do it His way. The Bride of Christ really can prepare herself for His return.

The message of this writing—and the message of Christianity as a whole—is not negative. It is not a *no*. It is a *yes*. "All God's promises are yes in Christ" (2 Corinthians 1:20)! But we will never experience the richness and blessings of the future until we look honestly at the present. We must evaluate the fruit of what we are currently doing. And we must be willing to put our preconceptions and biases on the table as well, so that they can be evaluated in the light of God's truth.

Albert Einstein once said that the definition of insanity is "doing the same thing over and over again while expecting different results." We dare not be guilty of such madness! What we do must change; who we *are* must change. All illusions of "peace, peace where there is no peace" must change first. We must reject self-satisfaction or complacency.

Let's go back to our survey of pastors and quote from the pollster's own conclusions:

> When pastors described their notion of significant, faith-driven life change, the vast majority (more than four out of five) focused on salvation but ignored issues related to lifestyle or spiritual maturity. The fact that the lifestyle of most churched adults is essentially indistinguishable from that of unchurched people is not a concern for most churches; whether or not people have accepted Jesus Christ as their savior is the sole or primary indicator of "life transformation," regardless of whether their life after such a decision produces spiritual fruit…It's a bit troubling to see pastors feel they're doing a great job when the research reveals that few congregants have a

biblical worldview, half the people they minister to are not spiritually secure or developed, kids are fleeing from the church in record numbers, most of the people who attend worship services admit they did not connect with God, the divorce rate among Christians is no different than that of non-Christians, only 2% of the pastors themselves can identify God's vision for their ministry they are trying to lead, and the average congregant spends more time watching television in one day than he spends in all spiritual pursuits combined for an entire week. Pastors, alone, cannot be held accountable for the spiritual disrepair of America. But it's worrisome when there is a strong correlation between church size and self-satisfaction, because that suggests that attendance and budget figures have become our mark of success. It's troubling when our spiritual leaders cannot articulate where we're headed and how the Church will fulfill its role as the restorative agent of our society. Maybe the comfort afforded by our buildings and other material possessions has seduced us into thinking we're farther down the road than we really are.[17]

We may not have all the answers. But we can at least begin by admitting that we need them!

Jesus says that in His Kingdom, good teaching produces good fruit. If our teaching by and large hasn't, then we need to make some sweeping changes. "New" or "exotic" doctrines are not needed. The answers won't come in some extra-biblical revelation. The core message of Christianity always has been and always must be "Christ, and Him crucified." We are obligated to "contend for the faith once delivered to the saints."

We are not advocating new doctrines; we *are* advocating a renewed commitment to following the instructions and example of Jesus and His apostles, as recorded in the New Testament. Please read that precious document with fresh eyes. Ask yourself these questions: What was the *starting point* of the apostle's teaching, when they were reaching out to those who were just being confronted with the claims of Jesus? What was the *emphasis* of their teaching, when they were instructing believers in how to grow up in the faith? And what was the *context* or *environment* of their teaching? We urge you to explore apostolic writings for yourself. May these words stimulate and provide direction for your search!

8

RIGHT HERE, RIGHT NOW!

Imagine Once More...

Imagine your planet. It is still fallen. You are still waiting for the day when "every knee shall bow and every tongue confess that Jesus Christ is Lord." But here and there, invading the cities and towns and villages scattered around the globe, are outposts of heaven's life. They are *ekklesias*. Let's take an imaginary spiritual snapshot of the planet. If we pick a moment in time and zoom in on four of these divine outposts, what might we see?

—■—■—■—

The city is just waking up. To the east, the sun inches over the horizon, bathing the foothills with a rose-colored dawn. To the west, the Canadian Rockies are barely visible against the still darkened sky. The five men in the living room are oblivious to the morning's beauty. Instead, their hearts are glimpsing the splendor of heavenly realms. They are huddled on their knees. In a few minutes, two of the men will hop on the train into the city to the large chemical plant where one of them works as an accountant and the other as a research technician. Another will drive his car to a large retail store nearby, where he works as the manager. The two young men are students at the university. Neither has a class until the afternoon. They don't have to be up so early, but they want to be in that room. Like the others in the huddle, they sense *life* when they are together with the brothers and sisters. That life can happen any time in any place, but this morning, for these five men at least, it is happening in this room.

This particular gathering came together rather spontaneously the night before, when one of the men asked if some guys could pray with him about challenges at work. When they arrived an hour ago, they grabbed a quick breakfast and began to talk quietly. One of the brothers shared an encouraging scripture; another told of what he had learned during a similar experience at his own job. Now they are on their knees, praying first about the brother's challenging day. But their simple petitions quickly change to a sincere thanksgiving in words of praise that are free from religious jargon. Inside each man's heart, the "Morning Star" has risen, just like the sun!

—■—■—■—

We zoom in on another outpost eight time zones to the east. The sun, just past its peak in the clear sky, sends its shimmering heat on the small city below. In this Mediterranean country, the mid-afternoon is a time for rest. Shops and businesses close for a couple of hours. The employees head home for their main meal of the day and some welcome relaxation. They will return to their offices and shops soon and will work into the evening. For now, they rest. But the brothers and sisters of a local *ekklesia* in this city have discovered that mid-afternoon is an ideal time to gather. Often they congregate in small groups in their homes, sharing food and encouragement and song. Today, however, some of the brothers put the word out that everyone should meet at a small park near the center of town. So it is that while the five men are praying in the living room in Canada, a considerably larger group of believers has converged on a park in southern Spain.

The streets are quiet, so the gathering attracts little notice besides an occasional curious look from a passerby. The believers are content to have a moment of relative anonymity. Over the past few years, they have been the subject of escalating rumors and criticisms in the city. Traditions run strong in this culture. Some are literally thousands of years old. So when a group of people decide to live their lives differently, some neighbors and co-workers and family members feel a bit threatened. The *ekklesia* has been feeling the weight of some especially ugly opposition lately. That's why a few of the brothers decided it would be wise to take advantage of the mid-day break and gather everyone for some needed encouragement and vision. Each person or household brought food to share. Someone prepared unleavened bread and wine, so they have spent much of their first hour remembering Jesus' sacrifice for them, reminding each other why they love Him, and thanking Him for loving them first.

Now someone opens a Bible and begins to read 1 Peter. They read about their "new birth into a living hope" because of the "precious blood of Christ," about how He is a "living Stone—rejected by men but chosen by God and precious to Him," and about how they, too, are "living stones, being built into a spiritual house to be a holy priesthood." They read about "suffering as a Christian," "repaying evil and insult with blessing," about "being prepared to give an answer," and about "the Spirit of glory and of God resting on them" when they are "insulted for the name of Christ." Spirits begin to soar in the Spanish park, just as they are soaring in the Canadian living room!

At that precise moment, two men are walking together steadily towards the main crossroads in an African town. They pass by the small open air market where they set up shop most mornings, selling eggs and sometimes chickens from their small poultry operation. They smile and nod at several of their fellow believers and continue walking. They know their brothers and sisters are praying for them. Right now they are partners in something much dearer to their hearts than their business. At the town's main intersection is its only petrol station, which services any vehicles that pass through—the occasional truck or government car or tourist's van. It is also a prime location for the town's beggars to gather, in hopes that a tourist will hand them a coin or a bit of food. The two men walking to the petrol station are looking for one specific beggar. They saw him for the first time yesterday. He was a newcomer—a young boy, perhaps eight years old, with a huge, ugly white scar on his forehead. Yesterday, he had said nothing—only motioned at his mouth to show that he was hungry. They had given him the only food they had, their lunches for the day. He had flashed a grateful smile at them and run off. As the day went on, the men had frequently spoken about the boy. They had seen beggars before. But there was something about this boy. One image they simply couldn't get out of their minds was his filthy, ragged tee-shirt, decorated with a sneering caricature of the devil and a blasphemous phrase. It was probably the only shirt he had worn for months, if not years. Last night, the men had called the *ekklesia* together to ask Jesus for wisdom about what to do with that boy. The gifts of the Body were evident that night—discernment, helps, generosity, leadership, teaching. Someone finally put into words what they all seemed to be thinking. Everyone nodded and smiled and clapped.

So today, the two men are going back to the petrol station to find that boy. They are carrying a parcel of fish and rice, along with a clean white shirt. They will speak with him today. And if they find out that he is an orphan or an abandoned child, as they suspect, they have something else to offer him: a new home.

Six times zones farther to the east is a nation of islands. The sun has long since set in the direction of the Asian mainland, but a group of several dozen believers—old and young, male and female—are gathered on the beach. Overhead, the tropical night sky puts on a display of sparkling beauty, but the group scarcely notices. They are focused on the silhouettes of a man and a woman wading out a few meters from the shore. The man is a trusted brother, a strong but gentle leader who has been known to take courageous stands in the shanty-town community where most of the *ekklesia* lives. Like most places on our planet, this nation is steeped in religious tradition. This *ekklesia* has received its share of opposition and slander.

Some of the antagonism has been coming from the woman who is now wading out into the water. Her biological sister has been reborn for a year now. To her family, it has felt like a betrayal of their heritage. The more the new Christian has spoken of her faith in Jesus, the angrier her parents and siblings have become. The most vocal critic has been the woman who is now up to her waist in the warm waters of the Mindanao Sea. She has been the source of vicious rumors, accusing the members of the shanty-town *ekklesia* of exploiting and abusing her sister. The slander has hurt many. The new Christian herself has essentially been driven out of her parents' house and is now living with a young couple in the *ekklesia*.

A short time ago, however, the angry sister's infant son became seriously ill with a bad fever. The woman and her husband watched hopelessly over the next week as their baby's condition deteriorated. In desperation, the woman went to her Christian sister, begging for prayer. The young woman brought six members of the *ekklesia* with her, including the older brother who is also now standing in the water by the baby's mother. Together, they prayed for the infant. In fact, they knelt around his little bed far into the night. Finally, in a dark hour after midnight, the boy's fever broke. The next morning his appetite returned, along with the sparkle in his eyes. The woman broke down in tears, kissing the hands and feet of the believers who had interceded in heavenly realms for her child. Over the next few days, the believers had shared the good news of Jesus with the family, a Jesus who is *alive* and well and accessible to His people: Immanuel, "God with us."

The woman now is surrendering her life to this Jesus. Her husband also seems "not far from the Kingdom." Standing in the water, she renounces her life of selfishness and sin, asking Jesus to forgive her for persecuting Him. She confesses Him as Lord. The man standing next to her "buries" her in the water, then "raises" her to walk a new life. The assembled *ekklesia* bursts into song!

—■—■—■—

Does this snapshot of twenty-first century *ekklesia* life look good to you? It should—you were born for it, if indeed you have been "born from above"! We realize that if you are like most people, your existence doesn't look very similar to these pictures. We also realize that you can't just snap your fingers and change your environment to look like what we have described. But do you *long* for it?

Imagine and Ask!

If you want to experience a "right here, right now" life with Jesus in His *ekklesia*, the place to begin is *not* with the latest religious movement or fad. Sorry! You are free to try if you want, but we're here to tell you that it just won't work. The Kingdom of God isn't built that way.

The first Eden, when man and woman walked and talked with God in humble submission and trust, wasn't produced by a religious movement or a five-step program. Man creates programs; God creates Eden. Genesis 1 is a majestic, sweeping portrait, painted with broad, vibrant brush strokes, of a God who by His own counsel decided to create an entire universe out of nothing. He chose to plant a Garden on one planet and place the man and woman in it. He decided to come to that Garden and walk with them. After the fall, mankind tried (once) to "build a tower to the heavens." Man's first "program" had high ambitions, but it failed miserably. God made certain it did.

The second "Garden" experience, when men and women walked and talked with God on the dusty roads of Palestine, was also His sovereign act. No one brought Christ to earth. "Do not say in your heart, 'Who will ascend into heaven?' (that is, to bring Christ down)" (Romans 10:6). Instead, Jesus, "being in very nature God, did not consider equality with God something to be grasped, but made Himself nothing, taking the very nature of a servant, being made in human likeness" (Philippians 2:6-7). Jesus came of His own volition. His love and humility brought Him into fellowship with man once more.

The third "Eden," when people enjoyed intimacy with God once more within the *ekklesia*, likewise was His creation. The first church was not produced by religious zeal; in fact, religion opposed it relentlessly. It came into being when Jesus sovereignly poured out His Spirit on mankind. This was no "church planting," informed by the marketing principles of the church growth movement and equipped with the latest in religious technology. What we call Pentecost happened when an "unschooled, ordinary" man stepped forward to explain that he and his friends didn't have a drinking problem—and a few minutes later, three thousand people pledged their all to follow an executed felon. The church was birthed by Holy Spirit power. No program, however well intentioned, has ever been more than a cheap imitation of God's sovereign might.

"I will build My church," Jesus has declared. He has built before. He can build again.

After all, the church was God's idea! "His intent was that now, *through the church*, the manifold wisdom of God should be made known to the rulers and authorities in the heavenly realms, according to His eternal purpose which He accomplished in Christ Jesus our Lord" (Ephesians 3:10-11).

God's surprising intention is to demonstrate His wisdom through redeemed human beings, joined together through intimate relationship with each other and with Him. God's wisdom is manifold. It is a jewel with countless facets. Somehow, someway, the network of relationships in the *ekklesia* is to demonstrate each facet of that jewel. The "rulers and authorities in the heavenly realms" are quite accustomed to the sad spectacle of a humanity that is "foolish, disobedient, deceived and enslaved by all kinds of passions and pleasures," living "in malice and envy, being hated and hating one another" (Titus 3:3). But when the rulers and authorities see an example of redeemed humanity joined by bonds of love and devotion and humility, they take notice, and they marvel at God's wisdom that He could conceive and accomplish such a miracle.

And so it is *right* to imagine God's *ekklesia*, as we have done. What is even more right is to *ask* Him to accomplish His intent in your city and around the globe. "Now to Him who is able to do immeasurably more than all we ask or imagine, according to His power that is at work within us, to Him be glory in the church and in Christ Jesus throughout all generations, forever and ever! Amen" (Ephesians 3:20-21).

God's intent is to build the church. He invites you to imagine and ask Him to accomplish His purpose on planet earth, including the nation and city where you live. His plan is to do *immeasurably more* than you are capable of asking, not by "blessing" some movement or program in some external way, but by working *within* His people.

So imagine…and ask!

The Kingdom of God is Within You

When Adam and Eve fell, there was serious harm done to the material universe. It was cursed with thorns, pain, and death. But the greatest damage of all was done *inside* human beings. They had wanted independence from God, and they got it. Their hearts, which once had been brimming with trust and love and submission, were now overflowing with pride and fear and alienation. If we want to return to the Eden-life of walking with God, it is this inner damage that first must be undone.

The *ekklesia* is an inner Kingdom:

> Once, having been asked by the Pharisees when the kingdom of God would come, Jesus replied, "The kingdom of God does not come with your careful observation, nor will people say, 'Here it is,' or 'There it is,' because the kingdom of God is within you." (Luke 17:20-21)

In the *ekklesia*, the curse is reversed. It is a realm men enter only when they renounce their independence from God and acknowledge their deep, deep need of Him. Instead of compartmentalizing their lives into the "sacred" and the "secular," they bring all of life under His authority and blessing. Instead of vainly trying to meet with God in a temple made of stone, they meet with Him in a dwelling made of submitted human lives. In the *ekklesia*, men and women "unmake" the horrible decision that Adam and Eve made in the Garden, and which truthfully we have each made in our own lives. In the *ekklesia*, people go back to the fork in the road, but this time they choose the road less traveled by.

There was a time when people didn't "get religion" by repeating a rote prayer or mentally agreeing to a set of principles. "Conversion" was viewed as changing kingdoms. It was renouncing one set of loyalties and embracing another. It was being "buried with Christ" in His death and "raised to live a new life" in His resurrection. It meant being a different person, a new creation.

Has that experience been yours? Have you been cut to the heart when you learned that God made "this Jesus, whom you crucified, both Lord and Christ"? Have you rejected the old way of being in control of your own time, money, relationships, and priorities? Have you placed all of those things under Jesus' control? Have you entered into a relationship of loving trust with Him, so that when you do disappoint Him, the first thing you want to do is run back to Him and lose your life in Him again?

If that hasn't been your life, it can be now!

That is the only way you can "walk with God in the cool of the day." The experience Adam and Eve enjoyed with their Creator in Eden, or that Peter and James and John and Mary Magdalene enjoyed with Jesus in Galilee, or that thousands of redeemed men and women experienced with Jesus and with one another in the early church, can be yours. But it can only happen if you personally reject the way of independence—reject even *religious* self-sufficiency—and return to the state of heart you were created for.

Any "church" that isn't based on each member having Jesus rule in their hearts as King is not the *ekklesia* we read about in the New Testament. In the final analysis, it doesn't matter if you have the most informal, friendliest, least traditional life-style of any religious assembly on earth. If the Kingdom of God isn't within you, what you have isn't the Kingdom of God.

So begin there. Imagine the *ekklesia*. Ask God for it. And position yourself to be a part of it by submitting your own heart to His reign. Then call others to do the same!

Kingdom Seeds

The "Kingdom of God is within" the hearts of people who have truly received Him there as King. Hopefully, you are one of those people. And hopefully, you realize that you need the Spirit that has been deposited in other hearts as well. It is the interconnected network of relationships that constitutes the "holy place" where you can walk with God.

Imagine a beautiful mosaic portrait of Jesus. It is a masterpiece, capturing the courage, tenderness, humility, nobility, authority, and love in His face. Any individual tile by itself conveys very little of the portrait. Each tile makes its contribution, but they need each other, and they need to be joined by the hand of a master to create the picture.

That mosaic is the church. As Paul wrote, "We [plural] are God's workmanship"—literally, His masterpiece—"created in Christ Jesus" (Ephesians 2:10). If you are born again, you are one of those tiles. Christ is in you, your "hope of glory." But the image of Christ you can portray in isolation is very limited. The Holy Spirit has deposited a gift, some aspect of Jesus, uniquely in you. But for the full picture to emerge, you need to be placed side-by-side with other "tiles." That's the only way that you and they can experience Jesus' presence in a full, complete way or demonstrate His presence before an unbelieving world.

Jesus commanded us, "Love one another. As I have loved you, so you must love one another. By this all men will know that you are my disciples, if you love one another" (John 13-34-35). When Jesus came to earth, He rejected the temptation to demonstrate His greatness to the unbelieving world through some impressive publicity stunt, such as casting Himself off the temple roof. He knew His Father's will. He understood that God's intent was to demonstrate His manifold wisdom "now, through the church." Jesus lined up His heart fully with His Father's. He invested His energies, not in proving Himself through impressive displays of miraculous might, but in building a church—a network of loving relationships.

The love Jesus spoke of—the *agape* of New Testament Greek— wasn't some shallow feeling or fleeting emotion. It was a practical, dynamic devotion and dedication to seeking the good of another person, *despite* any feelings or emotions to the contrary! Jesus demonstrated that life day in, day out, for forty months with His disciples. He fed them, taught them, rebuked them, forgave them, and washed their feet. He opened His life wide to them. He denied Himself comfort and privacy and preferences just to be with them. He laid down His own legitimate needs to meet *their* needs. And then, after three and a half years of demonstrating that *agape*, Jesus called on them to live that way with each other. Only then could God's wisdom be manifested "now, through the church."

That is your mission, should you choose to accept it: to lay your life down for others as Jesus did.

Of course, many genuinely re-born people find themselves very much in the position of that tile we spoke of, whose colors are bright and true, but who isn't joined side-by-side with other tiles in any meaningful way. There may be other tiles around you, but it's hard to be sure who they are. You can't really tell what another person is made of just by staring at the back of his or her head in the pew in front of you once or twice a week, or by watching him or her raise hands and sway with a worship song, or even by hearing his or her insightful comment in the "house church" living room. What are you to do?

You have to begin somewhere. And if you haven't "begun" already, what are you waiting for? Like Jesus, you need to deny yourself and open your life wide, making room for others in it. You're going to have to ignore all the instincts of your flesh and begin de-compartmentalizing your life! It's not that you need to "get more committed" and dedicate more hours to your "church life" at the expense of your "family life" or "devotional life" or "work life." It's that you must begin to *merge your worlds* into a single life!

Practically, you must begin rearranging your priorities and habits so that other people can fit in. Is there a way to get face-time with brothers or sisters during daily life? Can you arrange car-pooling or lunch hours to be with believers? Can you do the shopping or banking or other errands with another disciple this time? Can you go to the little league game where your friend coaches, and his son plays ball? Can you even volunteer to help out? Can you sign your child up for the same soccer league that the child of a believer plays in, even if it means a few minutes extra driving? Are you willing to do these or a thousand other "little" things to begin de-compartmentalizing your life, and to begin merging your world with someone else's? And as you are opening up your life, will you open your heart as well? Will you be vulnerable, confessing your sins and asking for prayers as the Bible says? Will you risk, asking caring questions about genuine concerns you have about your brothers' and sisters' lives? And will you take the time to help them?

Of course, it goes without saying that "it takes two" or more for this "dance." One sad heritage from the history of Christendom is that almost everyone *claims* to be a Christian. Despite overwhelming evidence to the contrary, every country in the Western world thinks of itself as a "Christian nation." Scientific surveys conducted by the Gallup and Barna groups in recent years bear witness to these facts. Nearly nine of ten Americans (88%) say they feel "accepted by God." Almost all of them (84%) claim to be Christians. A huge majority of Americans (72%) claim they have made "a personal commitment to Jesus Christ that is important in their life today." Most American adults (62%) feel that they are not only religious, but "deeply spiritual." They think religion is "very important" in their own personal lives and say that they "believe that religion can answer all or most of today's problems." Two-thirds say they belong to a religious assembly of some sort. At least half attend services nearly every week. Half of all Americans say they've been "born again or had a born-again experience"—that is, a "turning point in their lives when they committed themselves to Jesus Christ."

The sad truth is that most of these people are wrong. We aren't being judgmental; we're only stating the obvious. Think about it: over a *quarter of a billion* Americans think they are Christians and fine with God. But according to Jesus Himself, they simply can't all be right. *In fact, most of them have to be wrong.* If "wide is the gate and broad is the road that leads to destruction, and many enter through it," it is inconceivable that only a tiny fraction of one of the most populous nations on earth are on that broad road. And if "small is the gate and narrow the road that leads to life, and only a few find it," than most of the hundreds of millions who believe they are on that narrow road are quite tragically mistaken.

So don't be discouraged if many of the people you invite into your life say, "No thanks." And don't give up if the ones who initially seem enthusiastic later wither away when the going gets tough, or if others can't really find the time amid their own personal obsessions with life's riches, worries, and pleasures. Jesus said a lot of people were going to be that way (Luke 8:1-15). So when you run into folks like that—and you will—you're going to have to have the courage and discernment to move on. Maybe things will change in the future; you'd love it if they would. But for now, you need to sow the seeds of the Kingdom as widely as you're able with the people in your environment.

You can't control the choices others make, but you can control your own. And you can begin pleading with God for the emergence of His *ekklesia* and positioning your life to be a part, by erasing the compartmentalization and inviting others in.

Raising Vision

For the rest of your days, you can devote yourself to raising vision in the people around you. Your vision for what is called "the Christian life" or "the church" need not be limited by what you have personally seen or experienced. The spark of faith in your own heart need not—indeed, must not—be extinguished by someone else's low vision in this or any other century. Your vision should not even be limited by what the first-century church experienced. Consider their faith in and experience of Jesus, then aim for something higher—and settle for nothing less—than what they lived out.

God's word sets the standard. Make stepping into the life described there your goal. Set the bar at that level and refuse to lower it. Don't let your failures, inabilities, poor track record, or questions *talk you out of believing God*. "Let God be true and every man a liar."

His word describes a church where His gifts "prepare God's people for works of service, so that the body of Christ may be built up until we all reach unity in the faith and in the knowledge of the Son of God and become mature, attaining to the whole measure of the fullness of Christ" (Ephesians 4:12-13). That's right—it says "the *whole* measure of the *fullness* of Christ"! There is an entire universe of potential in that phrase. But it needs to become reality on planet earth. And God's word says that it can!

Jesus spoke of a church that overcomes persecution, betrayal, hatred, and deception. It "stands firm to the end" and even "takes the gospel of the Kingdom as a testimony to all nations" *before* the end comes (Matthew 24:4-14). He said that He would build a church that could bust down the very gates of hell (Matthew 16:18). Whether you or I have seen such a church doesn't change what Jesus said. The only begotten Son of God was never wrong!

The last book of the Bible foretells a wedding between the Lamb and His bride, the church:

> Hallelujah! For our Lord God Almighty reigns. Let us rejoice and be glad and give Him glory! For the wedding

> of the Lamb has come, and His bride has made herself
> ready. Fine linen, bright and clean, was given her to wear.
> (Fine linen stands for the righteous acts of the saints.)
> (Revelation 19:6-8)

That church is coming. You may not be able to mark it on your calendar, but you can mark it in your heart. Are you the kind of person who "looks forward to the day of God and speeds its coming"? Then you are also someone who can live "a holy and godly life" in preparation for it (2 Peter 3:11-12). You can trust God and ask Him diligently to ready His church for that day. You can fully surrender your own heart and will and life to Him, welcoming Him to reign as Lord over each moment. You can reach out and learn to love others. And you can nurture in your heart— and in the hearts of everyone around you who will listen—a vision for what God wants to accomplish on this planet, "now, through the church."

In practical terms, you can share these and other scriptures with those around you and call them to pledge themselves to see the words become reality. You can share carefully selected books or recorded teachings that will also cast a vision for a genuine walk with Jesus in the church.[18] And you can watchfully, with wisdom and diligence, explore relationships with brothers and sisters in other cities or nations who share your vision for experiencing Jesus in the *ekklesia*.

If we may offer you our unsolicited advice: steer clear of anyone who wants you to join something or who "peddles the Word of God for profit." Do not jump on a bandwagon that encourages you to abandon your responsibilities of helping the people you already know in the place where you already live. And it hopefully goes without saying that if you surf chat rooms and bulletin boards in search of "Christian fellowship," you are "looking for love in all the wrong places." Still, you do need relationships with people who will help you keep your own vision raised as you in turn help others. So reach out!

Seeking a Better City

The first-century *ekklesias* were born through suffering. Paul wrote something quite remarkable to the Colossians: "I am glad when I suffer for you in my body, for I am participating in the sufferings of Christ that continue for His body, the church" (Colossians 1:24). Just before He died, Jesus declared, "It is finished." His sufferings and death on the cross were overwhelmingly more than enough to pay the price for all of our sins. To secure our salvation, no other sacrifice will ever be necessary. Yet to establish and build up the church, much pain is still required. Jesus still suffers today for the church, but now He suffers in the bodies of men and women whose hearts are His home.

Dear reader, this means you. Jesus will build His *ekklesia*. But if you want to "serve the purposes of God in your generation," there is a price that you personally must pay.

Part of that price is persecution. Paul told Timothy, "Everyone who wants to live a godly life in Christ Jesus will be persecuted" (2 Timothy 3:12). To experience persecution, you don't have to become an apostle and travel to some foreign land. All you have to do is *desire* to live a godly life, and you will be guaranteed to experience harassment and maltreatment.

Persecution will happen to you, and when it does, it will not make sense. It will seem so unfair. It will be impossible to fathom how someone could *believe* the slander and rumors and gossip about you, let alone *start* them. You will find yourself lying awake at night, staring at your bedroom ceiling, begging God to show you what you did to deserve this pain, and crying out to Him for the strength to go forward.

There's nothing anyone can write in a book that will make it feel any better when it happens. Just be prepared, as best as you can; it will happen. And run into Jesus' arms when it does. Be humble enough to learn from your mistakes, but don't be crippled by them. Correct what needs correction in your life, but reject the temptation to blame yourself for everything. Opposition doesn't mean that you've failed; it very well could mean that you are doing something right. At the very least it can mean that you sincerely desire to live a godly life in Christ Jesus—and that's not such a bad thing, is it?

When persecution happens, search the scriptures for how to handle it. (Jesus and Peter and John all gave really good advice on the topic!) Dive into the Psalms of David; they will come to life for you as never before. Pray. Remember that your enemies are not flesh and blood; they are the spiritual forces of evil in the heavenly realms. Don't lash out against flesh and blood. Fight back against those spiritual forces of evil; hit *them* where it hurts, by embracing faith, hope and love in your heart and continuing to sacrifice your time and passion and energy and life for the *ekklesia*. That is, after all, what the enemy is trying to put a stop to.

Write this phrase on your heart in preparation for that day: "So then, those who suffer according to God's will should commit themselves to their faithful Creator and continue to do good" (1 Peter 4:19). In the final analysis, that's the only response worth having.

Of course, most of your "participation in the sufferings of Christ that continue for His body, the church" won't take the form of persecution. When Paul listed the "troubles, hardships and distresses" that commended him as a servant of Christ, he did mention "beatings, imprisonments and riots." But that wasn't all! He quickly added "hard work and sleepless nights" to the list and concluded that he was "sorrowful, yet always rejoicing; poor, yet making many rich; having nothing, and yet possessing everything" (2 Corinthians 6:3-10). Most of the suffering you experience for the sake of the *ekklesia* will be of that kind.

Whether you are sowing seeds for the future or experiencing the *ekklesia* in present reality, much of your suffering will come down to nitty-gritty decisions of self-denial. Will you give up that quiet evening you were looking forward to for the sake of someone who is hurting and needs encouragement and help? Will you fast for others? Will you stay up late or get up early to pray for them? Will you have the courage to go to others when you have concerns about their lives? Will you have the humility to listen to others when they have concerns about yours? Will you share financial resources to help brothers and sisters who are overburdened? Will you deny yourself your preferences—favorite foods, preferred entertainment, tidy living room—to make a place in your life where others can fit in? A life built from such small decisions will never earn you a prominent place in future editions of the "Book of Martyrs," but they will position you for a place in the church Jesus is building.

Your motives will be tested! If you want relationships for their own sake, the whole experience will eventually turn sour for you. The "alternative Christian lifestyle" that you dream of will be outside your reach. If you are spiritually ambitious, wanting to be in on "God's cutting edge end-time movement" and go down in history as "doing great things for God," you will fail—and likely take your place among the persecutors of the *ekklesia*. But if you simply want to take up your cross daily and follow Jesus, how can you "fail" at that? That kind of life isn't a question of "success" or "failure"; it's a matter of trust and obedience and resiliency. If there's something you want to get out of it, you can (and hopefully will) fail. But if you are simply trying to obey the two greatest commandments— loving God with all you've got and loving others desperately and self-sacrificially—no person or thing on earth can stop you.

Whatever role God means for you to play will require perseverance on your part. You'll have to keep right on obeying Him, even if it doesn't seem like it's "working." As the Hebrews writer said, you must continue being "sure of what you hope for and certain of what you do not see." You must imitate the examples of faith who have gone before you:

> All these people were still living by faith when they died. They did not receive the things promised; they only saw them and welcomed them from a distance. And they admitted that they were aliens and strangers on earth. People who say such things show that they are looking for a country of their own. If they had been thinking of the country they had left, they would have had opportunity to

return. Instead, they were longing for a better country—a heavenly one. Therefore God is not ashamed to be called their God, for He has prepared a city for them. (Hebrews 11:13-16)

So persevere! Refuse to sell out. Refuse to be coerced or shamed or bribed or frightened into silence. Keep pressing forward. Keep seeking the better city!

—■—■—■—

"Therefore, my dear brothers, stand firm. Let nothing move you. Always give yourselves fully to the work of the Lord, because you know that your labor in the Lord is not in vain" (1 Corinthians 15:58).

"Let us not become weary in doing good, for at the proper time we will reap a harvest if we do not give up" (Galatians 6:9).

Amen. Come, Lord Jesus!

BIBLIOGRAPHY

Note: The points of view expressed in Right Here, Right Now! *are the author's own. The following sources provided factual information only. We warn the reader that many of the sources listed below are written by non-Christian scholars and may contain passages with offensive words or imagery.*

Aveni, Anthony F. *The Book of the Year: a Brief History of Our Seasonal Holidays.* New York: Oxford University Press, 2003.

Barna Update contributors, Barna Updates, http://www.barna. org. [Please note that The Barna Group has strict policies regulating the use of their statistics in for-profit publications. *Right Here, Right Now!* is never to be sold at any price; as the copyright indicates, it must always be distributed free of charge.]

Bellenir, Karen, ed. *Religious Holidays and Calendars: an Encyclopedic handbook.* Detroit: Omnigraphics, c2004

Carroll, J. W. How Do Pastors Practice Leadership? Research Report from Pulpit & Pew. Durham: Duke Divinity School, 2002.

Castelli, Elizabeth A. *Martyrdom and Memory: Early Christian Culture Making.* New York: Columbia University Press, 2004.

DeNavas-Walt, C., R. W. Cleveland, and B. H. Webster, Jr. Income in the United States: 2002. U.S. Census Bureau, September 2003.

Dennis, Matthew, ed. *Encyclopedia of Holidays and Celebrations: a Country-by-Country Guide.* New York: Facts on File, 2006.

Elliott, T. G. *The Christianity of Constantine the Great.* Scranton, PA: University of Scranton Press, 1996.

Fox, Robin Lane. *Pagans and Christians.* San Francisco: HarperSanFrancisco, 1995.

Garscoigne, Bamber. *Christianity: a history.* New York, NY: Carroll & Graf Publishers, 2003.

Henderson, Helene, ed. *Holidays, Festivals, and Celebrations of the World Dictionary: Detailing Nearly 2,500 Observances From All 50 States and More Than 100 Nations: a Compendious Reference*

Guide to Popular, Ethnic, Religious, National, and Ancient Holidays. Detroit, MI: Omnigraphics, 2005

Kalapos, Gabriella. *Fertility Goddesses, Groundhog Bellies & the Coca-Cola Company: the Origins of Modern Holidays.* Toronto: Insomniac, 2006.

Lee, A.D. *Pagans and Christians in Late Antiquity: a sourcebook.* New York: Routledge, 2000.

McMillan, B. R. "What do clergy do all week?" Research Report from Pulpit & Pew. Durham: Duke Divinity School, 2002

McMillan, B. R. and M. J. Price. How Much Should We Pay Our Pastor: A Fresh Look at Clergy Salaries in the 21st Century. Research Report from Pulpit & Pew. Durham: Duke Divinity School, 2003.

Moynahan, Brian. *The Faith: a History of Christianity.* New York: Doubleday, 2002.

Noll, Mark A. *Turning Points: Decisive Moments in the History of Christianity.* Grand Rapids, MI: Baker Books, 2000.

Travers, Len, ed. *Encyclopedia of American Holidays and National Days.* Westport, Conn.: Greenwood Press, 2006.

Wikipedia contributors. "Bahá'í Faith." *Wikipedia, The Free Encyclopedia.*

NOTES

[1] Please note that we are not advocating the "apprenticeship" model. Certainly these early believers recognized that only truly saved people should be regarded as members of the church, a priority that seems conspicuously lacking in most Christian circles in our era. Surely we can appreciate the very biblical concern of these early Christians for separation from the world (see, for example, 2 Corinthians 6:14-18) without imitating their rather legal and regimented implementation of this concern. At least they cared. Will we?

[2] It is a true irony of history that a few generations after Constantine, when the emperors of Rome abandoned the pagan religious title *pontifex* (English "pontiff"), the "bishops" of Rome began using it! The term is still used today by one religious body for the head of its leadership hierarchy.

[3] Jones, D. E., S. Doty, C. Grammich, J. E. Horsch, R. Houseal, M. Lynn, J. P. Marcum, K. M. Sanchagrin, and R. H. Taylor. *Religious Congregations and Membership in the United States 2000: An Enumeration by Region, State and County Based on Data Reported by 149 Religious Bodies,* Glenmary Research Center, 2002

[4] Barna Update, June 19, 2006

[5] Barna Update, January 8, 2007

[6] Socrates of Constantinople, *Historica Ecclesiastica*

[7] McMillan, B. R. "What do clergy do all week?" Research Report from Pulpit & Pew. Durham: Duke Divinity School, 2002

[8] McMillan, B. R. and M. J. Price. How Much Should We Pay Our Pastor: A Fresh Look at Clergy Salaries in the 21st Century. Research Report from Pulpit & Pew. Durham: Duke Divinity School, 2003.

[9] DeNavas-Walt, C., R. W. Cleveland, and B. H. Webster, Jr. Income in the United States: 2002. U.S. Census Bureau, September 2003.

[10] Carroll, J. W. How Do Pastors Practice Leadership? Research Report from Pulpit & Pew. Durham: Duke Divinity School, 2002.

[11] Barna Update, July 10, 2006

[12] The Barna Update, January 10, 2006

[13] Barna Update, October 22, 2002

[14] David Wilkerson newsletter, 2006

[15] Barna update, January 2, 2000

[16] Barna Update, September 8, 2004

[17] Barna Update, December 17, 2002

[18] This book, for example, will always be distributed free of charge. You have permission to copy it without changes and give it away to others. Together with many similar resources, this book will continue to be available in both electronic and hard copy formats from HeavenReigns.com, as God provides the resources. There will be no cost to you, nor will your donations ever be solicited or accepted. These materials are our offering to you and to Jesus.